# *Lease Financing*

# LEASE FINANCING
*A Practical Guide*

C. RICHARD BAKER, Ph.D., CPA

RICK STEPHAN HAYES

A RONALD PRESS PUBLICATION

JOHN WILEY & SONS　　New York • Chichester • Brisbane • Toronto

A portion of the material on leasing in this book has
been adapted from *Accounting, Finance and Taxation*
by C. Richard Baker and Rick Stephan Hayes,
published by CBT Publishing Company Inc., 51
Sleeper Street, Boston, Mass. 02210

*Library of Congress Cataloging in Publication Data:*

Baker, C. Richard, 1946–
    Lease financing, a practical guide.

    "A Ronald Press publication."
    Includes index.
        1.  Industrial equipment leases—Finance.
    I.  Hayes, Rick Stephan, 1946–     II.  Title.

HD39.4.B34     658.1'5242     81-576
ISBN 0-471-06040-2          AACR2

Printed in the United States of America

10 9 8 7 6 5 4 3 2 1

# CONTENTS

*Lease Financing*

# *Chapter 1*

# AN OVERVIEW
# OF LEASE FINANCING

This overview is intended for the reader who is unfamiliar with lease financing. The more sophisticated reader may proceed to subsequent chapters.

The general purpose of this book is to discuss lease financing as an alternative to the more traditional means of financing asset acquisitions. Leasing is a method available to a business of financing the acquisition of property. Under a lease arrangement, a leasing company or financial institution (the lessor) legally owns property that it in turn leases to another business firm (the lessee). The concept of leasing originated with large scale applications, such as the leasing of railroad rolling stock or special equipment leasing by companies that preferred leasing to selling (such as IBM or U.S. Shoe Machinery Corporation). Now a much broader scale of industry has evolved that leases everything from office machines to barges.

Instead of a lender and a borrower, as in a typical financing arrangement, in a lease arrangement there is a leasing company and its customer. Otherwise, the distinctions between ordinary borrowing arrangements and lease financing arrangements are not great.

We will discuss the advantages and disadvantages of leasing more thoroughly in a later chapter, but to summarize, the basic advantages of leasing are:

1  Facilitating the acquisition of needed equipment.
2  Making available funds that would otherwise be tied up in ownership of fixed assets.
3  Possible tax advantages.
4  Possible improvement of the statement of financial position (balance sheet).

These factors will be discussed later in this chapter.

## LEASING CREDIT CRITERIA, TERMS, AND RATES

Lease financing techniques and terms will differ depending on the lessor, the equipment or other assets leased, the length of the lease (i.e., lease term), and the prevailing interest rate. Following is a general discussion of lease rates and terms. (Lease finance is a technical subject involving many specialized definitions. See the Glossary at the end of the book.)

### Leasing Credit Requirements

The standards for granting credit to a lessee in a lease finance arrangement or to a borrower in a lending agreement are similar. The leasing company or financial institution is interested in the financial condition of the lessee and other pertinent business information. Generally, however, leasing companies are somewhat less strict than bank lenders when it comes to documentation and to financial strength of the lessee. Among the primary considerations of a leasing company are the intrinsic value (and marketability) of the equipment or property and the cash flow of the lessee.

### Leasing Contract Terms—Equipment

The majority of equipment leasing contracts range in term (length) from 2 to 10 years. Longer leases are usually special situations and call for lessees of excellent financial stature. Longer terms are also available to firms under special government-supported lease programs (such as the Small Business Administration Local Development Company, 502 lease program). Leases running less than 3 years are usually for rolling stock (trucks, forklifts, etc.) and office equipment (duplicators, computers, etc.). Many industrial equipment leases are written with 3 to 5 year terms. When we refer to the "term" of the lease we mean the "basic lease term," or the "initial" term of the lease. (See the Glossary at the end of the book.) After the initial term expires there are usually three alternatives:

1  Start a new lease with a new piece of property.
2  Purchase the property outright for some residual amount.
3  Renew the lease under an option that generally allows for reduced rent.

When a firm is leasing property that is rapidly changing in cost and efficiency (such as computers), the first alternative might be the right one. Under the second alternative, the lessee is given the opportunity to purchase the property at a price that will repay to the lessor the original cost of the property plus interest, less rents paid under the lease.

In many leasing contracts, the amount at which the property may be purchased from the lessor is called the residual value. However, Financial Accounting Standards Board Statement No. 13 (FASB No. 13), which contains the primary accounting rules dealing with leases (see Chapter 2), defines residual value as the fair market value of the property at the end of the lease term. We will define residual value in accordance with FASB No. 13 and use the phrase "residual purchase price" to mean the amount at which the property could be purchased from the lessor at the end of the lease term.

There are no set practices by which residual purchase prices are established, but a typical residual purchase price would be about 10 percent of the original cost of the equipment. The use of a fixed price purchase option may present problems because such options may remove some of the depreciation and investment tax credit incentives available to the lessor. The existence of a fixed price purchase option may prevent the classification of the lease arrangement as a "true lease" for tax purposes. (See definition in the Glossary and in Chapter 3.)

The third alternative would be exercised at the end of the initial lease term if doubt remained about whether to purchase the asset. Many renewal options provide for renewal term rents in the range of from 2 to 5 percent per year of the original list price of the equipment, as compared with initial term rents of from 4 to 11 percent per year of list price. Renewal term rental options may begin at 5 percent the first year and then drop thereafter. For example, if a piece of equipment having a value of $100,000 was leased to a company for 5 years, and if the company decided to renew the lease, the first year of the renewal period the rent may be $5000 per year. However, chances are that the lease would have cost the company in excess of $20,000 per year for the first 5 years it was under lease. Thus the first year's payment during the renewal period may be as much as $15,000 per year less than the payment during the original lease period. The reason for this reduced rent during the renewal period is obvious. The leasing company has received all of its original investment back and then some, so it can afford to keep the lease inexpensive for renewals.

Reduced rents in the renewal period pose certain accounting problems that will be addressed in Chapter 2.

## Lease Rates

Lease rates vary widely depending on the risk involved. Generally speaking, the more specialized the equipment or the longer the term of the lease, the higher the risk to the lessor.

A format that has been used frequently for determining lease rates is the add-on interest method. In the add-on method, the add-on percentage is multiplied by the contract term in years to get the total charge. For example, with a 5 percent add-on interest rate, for a $100,000 4 year lease, the add-on amount is $20,000 (4 × 5 percent of $100,000). The total payments under the lease would be $120,000. This is equivalent to a simple interest rate of 9.24 percent. If the leasing company used a simple interest rate of 5 percent on $100,000 for 4 years, the total of the payments over the 4 years would be $110,541 ($9459 less than with add-on interest of 5%). The add-on is often quoted as a separate increment to the contract. In other cases, the lease rate is quoted as a certain percentage of the original equipment cost per month (2 percent of the cost of the equipment per month is roughly equivalent to a 5 percent, 5 year, add-on interest rate).

When the lessee has a high credit rating, lease agreements may be written on a simple interest basis. The terms may range from 7 to 13 percent or higher simple interest. There are companies that offer better rates of interest. These arrangements are offered by leasing operations that are part of a larger enterprise that in turn will have substantial taxable income. Such companies have entered lease finance because, by legally owning the equipment they lease, they benefit from depreciation and investment tax credits. As a result of these tax savings, the interest rates charged may be below the rates for term loans. However, it should be noted that the lessee is giving up the tax benefits arising from depreciation and the investment tax credit. Therefore, leasing is primarily advantageous for a lessee who is unable to currently use depreciation deductions and investment tax credits. Subsidiaries of bank holding companies are likely to be participants as lessors in leases of this nature.

Some lessees may be concerned about not being able to purchase leased equipment or other property if they decide that ownership provides a better option than leasing. Other lessees may think they should be able to purchase the leased properties because they have already paid for it in the lease payments. In fact, no leasing company wants to wind up with equipment in its possession. Bank leasing companies, in particular, are in the business of leasing, not manufacturing, wholesaling, or retailing. As long as payments are made by the lessee, the leasing company will be satisfied, unless the leasing company has expectations of making a profit on the sale of the equipment at the end of the lease term. Therefore, it is probable that after the lease has run its course, the lessor will agree to sell the equipment. Lessees may be able to negotiate purchases midway through a lease contract. The provision for such a possibility usually cannot be prearranged or inserted into the lease contract as it could negate the treatment of the arrangement as a true lease for tax purposes. In addition, a lease agreement providing a purchase option that is clearly a bargain with respect to the fair value of the property may cause the lease to be capitalized on the books of the lessee. (See Chapter 2.)

Since new equipment is purchased from a manufacturer at a standard or normal price, this means that the leasing company is in essence making a 100 percent loan to the lessee. To reduce its risk, the lessor may require that the lessee put up a lease deposit. This lease deposit is usually equal to the first month's rent (lease payment) plus one additional month's rent for each year of the contract life of the lease. For example, a 5 year lease might call for a total deposit equivalent to 6 months' rent. The lessor may view this as a reserve; however, the lessor still has to make an advance of 100 percent of the market value of the leased equipment.

Some lessors will require only first and last months rent, but then require a "setup charge" or "security deposit" in addition to the rent advances.

## TYPES OF LEASES

### Sale-Leaseback

Under a sale-leaseback arrangement, a firm owning land, buildings, or equipment sells the property to a financial institution or other potential buyer-lessor and simultaneously executes an agreement to lease the property back for a specified period with specific terms.

In a sale-leaseback, the seller-lessee obtains the purchase price from the buyer-lessor immediately on sale. At the same time, the seller-lessee retains the use of the property. Under an alternative form of financing, such as a mortgage loan, the financial institution or bank would receive a series of payments sufficient to amortize the loan and provide the bank with a specified rate of return on its investment. Under a sale-leaseback arrangement, the lease payments are set up in a similar manner. The payments are sufficient to return the full purchase price to the buyer-lessor, in addition to providing the buyer-lessor with a stated return on its investment.

A variety of situations would be appropriate for sale-leasebacks. For example, a user of special metal presses may design and build its own presses, sell them to a leasing company at cost, and then lease them back. In business acquisitions, the acquiring company may have a leasing company buy the equipment of the company being acquired. The acquiring company then would lease the equipment back. A public utility company may sell and leaseback the electric turbines of its generating facility. Sale-leasebacks are increasingly becoming alternatives to traditional mortgage financing for large office buildings. (See Chapter 7.)

### Service Leases

Service leases include both financing and maintenance arrangements. IBM was one of the pioneers of the service lease. Xerox is another prime example. Computers, copiers, rolling stock, and vehicles (truck, cars, etc.) are the primary types of equipment involved in service leases.

An important characteristic of the service lease is the fact that it is frequently not full pay-out (i.e., the lease ends before the equipment is totally paid for). The lease contract is written for an initial term that is less than the expected life of the leased equipment. The lessor expects to recover his cost through subsequent renewal rental payments or through residual values on disposal of the leased equipment.

Service leases may contain a cancellation clause that provides the lessee with the right to cancel the lease and return the equipment before the expiration of the initial lease term. This is an important consideration for the lessee because the equipment may be returned if technological developments render the equipment obsolete.

## Net Lease or Finance Lease

A net lease is a lease that does not provide for maintenance services, is not subject to cancellation, and is full pay-out (i.e., the lessor receives rental payments equal to the full price of the leased equipment). The typical arrangement involves the following steps:

1  The firm that will use the equipment selects the specific items it desires and negotiates the price and delivery terms with the manufacturer or distributor.
2  The user firm arranges with a bank or leasing company to buy the equipment from the manufacturer or distributor, and the user firm simultaneously executes an agreement to lease the equipment from the financial institution. The terms call for full amortization of the financial institution's cost, plus a return on the unamortized balance. The lessee is generally given an option to renew the lease but will not have the right to cancel without completely paying off the financial institution.

Net finance leases are similar to sale-leasebacks except that the leased equipment is usually new and the lessor buys it from the manufacturer or distributor rather than from the user-lessee.

## TAX ASPECTS OF LEASING

There are potential tax advantages to leasing. However, leasing companies ordinarily will not make sweeping claims regarding such tax advantages.

To determine the character and type of tax deductions, a lessee must determine whether the lease agreement is a "true lease" or a "conditional sales contract." If the agreement is a true lease, the lessee may deduct rental payments for the use of the equipment or other property. If the agreement is a conditional sales contract (which means that the lessee has or will acquire legal title to the equipment or other property), the payments under the contract will be considered payments for the purchase of the property, and deductions will be allowed for depreciation and possibly interest expense. (See Chapter 3 for additional discussion.)

## Conditional Sales Contract

Ordinarily an agreement is considered a conditional sales contract (even if it is called a "lease"), and not a lease, if any of the following conditions are present:

1 Portions of the periodic payments are specifically applicable to an equity to be acquired by the "lessee."

2 Title will be acquired upon payment of a stated amount of "rentals" that the "lessee" is required to make under the contract.

3 The total payments required for a relatively short period of use constitute an excessively large portion of the total amount required to be paid to secure the transfer of the title to the equipment.

4 The agreed "rental" payments materially exceed the current fair market rental value for the same equipment. This may indicate that the payments include an element other than compensation for use of the equipment.

5 The property may be acquired under a purchase option at a price that is less than normal in relation to the value of the property at the time the option may be exercised, as determined at the time of entering into the original agreement, or that is relatively small when compared to the total payments the "lessee" is required to make.

6 Some portion of the periodic payments is specifically designated as interest or is otherwise readily recognizable as the equivalent of interest.

7 Title will be acquired on payment of an aggregate amount (e.g., the total of the rental payments plus the option price, if any) that approximates the initial sales price, plus interest and carrying charges, at which the "lessee" could have purchased the equipment when he entered into the agreement.

The following is an example of a lease treated as a sale:

Jones contracted for installation of a fire extinguishing sprinkler system in his warehouse. The system was estimated to last 20 years. The contract, designated as a lease, provided for use of the system for 5 years for an aggregate rental of $2000, payable $400 annually. The cost of the sprinkler system if purchased outright would have been $1900. Jones was required to keep the system insured for an amount at least equal to the total rentals and was to bear the risk of loss from any cause. The liability of the lessor in the event of failure of the system for any defect therein, or for maintenance services called for in the contract, was limited to $100. Jones had the privilege of renewal for three additional 5 year periods at a nominal rental of $20 a year.

This arrangement, for Federal income tax purposes, constitutes a conditional sale, rather than a lease. The amounts paid as rentals, except to the extent they represent interest, insurance repairs, and maintenance charges, are capital expenditures recoverable through annual deductions for depreciation over the estimated useful life of the sprinkler system.

Prior to FASB No. 13, which went into effect in 1977, the purpose of a lease arrangement, which for tax purposes was treated as a conditional sales contract, was to keep the liabilities arising from the installment sale off the lessee's balance sheet. Such leases were called "see through leases." Since the issuance of FASB No. 13, it has become more difficult to keep such lease arrangements off the balance sheet.

## Leveraged Leases

Certain leases are commonly referred to as leveraged leases. Such transactions involve three parties: a lessor, a lessee, and a lender to the lessor. Usually these are net finance leases (i.e., the lessee is responsible for all maintenance, insurance, and taxes). The lease term covers a large portion of the useful life of the leased property, and the lessee's payments to the lessor are sufficient to discharge the lessor's payments to the lender.

Parties to a transaction that appears to be leveraged lease may wish to consider securing an advance ruling from the Internal Revenue Service. Revenue Procedure 75-21, 1975-1 C.B. 715 (see Chapter 3) sets forth guidelines that are used for advance ruling purposes in determining whether leveraged leases are, in fact, leases for Federal income tax purposes. Among the guidelines are the following:

1  The lessor must have made a minimal unconditional at risk investment in the property.
2  The lessee may not have a contractual right to purchase the property from the lessor at less than fair market value at the time the right is exercised.
3  The lessee may not invest directly or indirectly in the property.
4  The lessee may not lend money to the lessor for investment purposes.
5  There must be a profit motive on the part of the lessor.

Other facts and circumstances in the lease arrangement may disqualify the transaction as a valid lease even though the guidelines have been met. See also Revenue Procedure 75-28, 1975-1 C.B. 752, for guidelines setting forth information and representations to be furnished by a taxpayer requesting an advance ruling in this area. (See Chapter 3.)

## Bona Fide Lease Transactions

The following is a summary of the principal requirements for a bona fide lease transaction from the standpoint of the IRS:

1  The term should be less than 30 years, otherwise the lease may be regarded as a form of sale.
2  The rent should represent a reasonable return to the lessor.
3  The renewal option should be bona fide. This requirement can best be met by giving the lessee the first option to meet an equal bona fide outside offer.
4  There should be no purchase option, or, if there is one, the lessee should merely be given parity with an equal outside offer.

## COMPARISON OF LEASING WITH OWNERSHIP

### Cost Comparison

For an understanding of the possible advantages and disadvantages of lease financing, the cost of leasing must be compared with the cost of owning. In the typical case, a firm that contemplates the acquisition of new equipment must also think about how to finance the equipment. To finance equipment there are at least three alternatives:

1  A lease agreement.
2  An installment sales contract.
3  A term loan secured by a chattel mortgage on the equipment.

To judge the cost of leasing it is necessary to compare leasing versus installment sales contracts and term loans. Exhibit 1.1 compares the alternatives. The exhibit assumes that the firm will acquire a piece of equipment costing $100,000 and that it has the choice of borrowing the $100,000 at 10 percent, to be repaid in 10 annual installments of $16,270, or of leasing the equipment for $16,270 per year with the investment tax credit passed through to the lessee.

**Exhibit 1.1** Comparison of Cost of Leasing with Ownership

|  | Year | | | | | | | | | | Total |
|---|---|---|---|---|---|---|---|---|---|---|---|
|  | 1 | 2 | 3 | 4 | 5 | 6 | 7 | 8 | 9 | 10 |  |
| **Ownership** | | | | | | | | | | | |
| (1) Debt Service | $16,270 | $16,270 | $16,270 | $16,270 | $16,270 | $16,270 | $16,270 | $16,270 | $16,270 | $16,270 | $162,700 |
| (2) Interest portion | 10,000 | 9,370 | 8,680 | 7,920 | 7,090 | 6,170 | 5,160 | 4,050 | 2,800 | 1,460 | 62,700 |
| (3) Tax benefits (46%) | 4,600 | 4,310 | 3,990 | 3,640 | 3,260 | 2,840 | 2,370 | 1,860 | 1,290 | 680 | 28,840 |
| (4) Depreciation | 10,000 | 10,000 | 10,000 | 10,000 | 10,000 | 10,000 | 10,000 | 10,000 | 10,000 | 10,000 | 100,000 |
| (5) Tax benefits (46%) | 4,600 | 4,600 | 4,600 | 4,600 | 4,600 | 4,600 | 4,600 | 4,600 | 4,600 | 4,600 | 46,000 |
| (6) Investment Tax Credit | 10,000 | — | — | — | — | — | — | — | — | — | 10,000 |
| (7) Net (cost) benefit of ownership (3) + (5) + (6) − (1) | 2,930 | (7,360) | (7,680) | (8,030) | (8,410) | (8,830) | (9,300) | (9,810) | (10,380) | (10,930) | $(77,860) |
| **Leasing** | | | | | | | | | | | |
| (8) Rent | $16,270 | $16,270 | $16,270 | $16,270 | $16,270 | $16,270 | $16,270 | $16,270 | $16,270 | $16,270 | $162,700 |
| (9) Tax Benefits (46%) | 7,480 | 7,480 | 7,480 | 7,480 | 7,480 | 7,490 | 7,490 | 7,490 | 7,490 | 7,490 | 74,840 |
| (10) Investment tax credit | 10,000 | — | — | — | — | — | — | — | — | — | 10,000 |
| (11) Net (cost) benefit of leasing | 1,210 | (8,790) | (8,790) | (8,790) | (8,790) | (8,780) | (8,780) | (8,780) | (8,780) | (8,780) | (77,860) |
| (12) Net benefit (cost) of ownership (7) − (11) | $ 1,710 | $ 1,430 | $ 1,110 | $ 760 | $ 380 | $ (50) | $ (520) | $ (1,030) | $ (1,600) | $ (2,190) | $ 0 |

Under the lease agreement, the firm is paying a 10 percent implicit interest rate, assuming no expectation of residual value on the part of the lessor.

In this example there is really no long-range advantage to leasing over ownership. Stated differently, in the long run, given the same payments for a lease as for purchase, there is no advantage to leasing. During the early years of operation, there are tax advantages to ownership. Over time, these advantages reverse and become negative compared with leasing in the later years of operation. If we assume inflation and the time value of money, savings in the early years of operation are worth more than savings in later years. Therefore, when we consider the time value of money, ownership offers advantages over leasing. (See Chapter 5.)

An additional advantage of ownership over leasing is the fact that with ownership the equipment belongs to the firm, and if the equipment has a value at the end of the lease, the equipment can be sold, potentially at a gain.

Nevertheless, the advantages of leasing may outweigh ownership in many cases, particularly when the lessee cannot take advantage of the tax benefits of ownership, or when a lease can be structured to provide off-balance sheet financing.

## Assumptions Commonly Made Regarding Cost of Leasing Versus Owning

Exhibit 1.2 summarizes some of the variations in leasing conditions and their assumed effect on leasing costs versus ownership costs. The exhibit summarizes advantages and disadvantages of leasing. Each assumed effect represented in the table is subject to qualification.

Each of these assumed conditions will be discussed in turn.

**Exhibit 1.2**  *Assumed Cost of Leasing Versus Ownership Under Various Conditions*

| | Cost of Leasing Versus Ownership | |
| --- | --- | --- |
| Condition | Lower | Higher |
| Firm uses accelerated depreciation | | X |
| Implicit interest rates are higher for leasing than for borrowing | | X |
| Equipment has large residual values | | X |
| Equipment experiences rapid obsolescence | X | |

*Use of Accelerated Depreciation*    It is argued that because of the ability to use accelerated depreciation methods, owning must be less expensive then leasing. This argument does not take into account the competitive aspects of the money and capital markets. Competition could force leasing companies to pass along tax advantages, such as accelerated depreciation and tax credits, to the lessee through reduced payments. The payment pattern for leasing can be quite flexible. Therefore, any opportunities available to lessors will probably be reflected in the competitive system of rates charged by leasing companies.

*Implicit Interest Rates Are Higher*    The statement is frequently made that leasing involves higher interest rates. This argument is doubtful. Generally when the nature of the lessee as a credit risk is considered, there should be little difference in the rates for nonleveraged finance equipment leasing from the rates for loans, especially when the tax aspects are taken into consideration. It is also difficult to separate the money costs of leasing from other services that may be embodied in a leasing contract. If the leasing company can perform nonfinancial services, such as maintenance of the equipment, at a lower cost than the lessee could perform such services, the effective cost of leasing may be lower than borrowing. The efficiencies of performing specialized services may enable the leasing company to operate by charging a lower total cost than the lessee would otherwise have to pay for the total package of services offered.

*Large Residual Values for Equipment*    The lessor rather than the lessee owns the property at the expiration of the lease. Therefore, it would appear that where residual values are expected to be high, owning will be less expensive than leasing. However, this advantage may be subject to qualification. With leased equipment, such as computers, or aircraft, obsolescence is an important factor. If residual values appear favorable, competition among leasing companies will probably force lease rates down to compensate for the large residual values involved. On the other hand, in connection with decisions whether to lease or to own land, the obsolescence factor will be negligible, and residual values are almost guaranteed. In a period of optimistic expectations about land values, prices may be overly inflated. Consequently, the current purchase of land may involve a price so high that the probable rate of return on owned land may be relatively small. Under this condition, leasing land may well represent an economical alternative. However, if the probable increase in land values is not fully reflected in current prices, it will be advantageous to own land.

*Rapid Obsolescence*    Another potential misconception is the belief that leasing costs will be lower because of rapid obsolescence of some kinds of equipment. If the obsolescence rate on equipment is high, leasing costs will reflect such factors. It is possible, however, that certain types of leasing companies may be well equipped to handle the obsolescence problem. For example, IBM is a manufacturer, reconditioner, and specialist in office equipment and has its own sales organization and system of distributors. This may enable IBM to write favorable leases on equipment. If the equipment becomes obsolete to one user, it may still be practical for another.

Leasing companies, by combining leasing with other specialized services, may reduce the cost of obsolescence and thereby increase residual values. Some special companies, through integrated operations, reduce the effective cost of leasing of equipment. Moreover, some institutions that do not combine leasing and other specialist functions, such as manufacturing, reconditioning, and servicing, may, in conjunction with financing institutions, perform the overall functions as efficiently as do integrated leasing companies.

## Cost of Capital Tied Up in Purchase

Although other techniques of property acquisition may cost less than leasing (a cash purchase without financing is the least expensive), such techniques represents only monetary savings on the financing of the purchase. Loss of the opportunity to make a profit on the capital that is required to be expended in a purchase may offset the savings of the purchase alternative. This is particularly true when the firm is making a good to excellent return on its investment. Assume for example that a firm is earning a 25 percent annual rate of return on its invested capital. If growth of the company requires the use of more capital, any money freed by leasing instead of purchasing theoretically could return 25 percent per annum to the company.

The money freed by leasing instead of purchasing generally represents the difference between the down payment that a firm would be required to make if it were financing and the rental deposits that would be required for leasing. Down payments are generally greater than deposits, so in the case of the aforementioned firm with a 25 percent return-on-investment, its return would represent 25 percent of the difference between the amount of the down payment and the amount of the lease deposit.

For example, for a piece of equipment worth $10,000 the down payment would generally be between 15 and 25 percent ($1500 to $2500). The lease deposit would be 10 month lease payments (first month plus one month for each year of the life of the contract). This would be $1322 if the equipment was worth $10,000 and there was an implicit interest rate of 10 percent per annum. All other things being equal, there would be $2000 in down payment to purchase and $1322 to lease. This means that the company has $678 available in capital for reinvestment. If the capital returned 25 percent per year, the company could make $1759 more by leasing instead of purchasing (assuming that the initial $678 was reinvested, with interest, each year for 10 years.)

## ACCOUNTING IMPLICATIONS OF LEASING

If leased property is regarded as property that is not owned by the lessee (i.e., an operating lease), the accounting treatment of a lease is simply to reflect the total lease payment as an expense. The lease would be recorded as follows:

**General Journal**

| Date | Transaction | Debit | Credit |
|------|-------------|-------|--------|
| 1/1/80 | Lease expense | $1600 | |
| | Cash | | $1600 |
| | To record monthly payment for a lease of a forklift truck from National Leasing Co. | | |

If the leased property is treated as property which is owned by the lessee (i.e. a capital lease), the accounting treatment of a lease is quite different. The lease would be recorded as follows:

**General Journal**

| Date | Transaction | Debit | Credit |
|------|-------------|-------|--------|
| 1/1/80 | Lease asset | $10,814 | |
| | Lease obligation | | $ 9214 |
| | Cash | | $ 1600 |
| | To record acquisition of a forklift truck under a 10 year noncancelable lease at $1600 per year with a discount rate of 10 percent. | | |

### Balance Sheet Implications

Two possibilities exist to maximize financial leverage through leasing under operating leases. First, it is possible for firms to obtain more money for longer terms under a lease arrangement than under a secured loan agreement for the acquisition of a given piece of equipment. Second, leasing may not have as much of an impact on future borrowing as would current borrowing. This point is illustrated by the following balance sheets from firms X and Y. Firm Y borrows $100,000 to buy equipment and Firm Y leases $100,000 worth of equipment under a operating lease. Their balance sheets are identical before the respective purchase or lease:

| | Before Equipment Purchase | After Equipment Purchase or Lease | |
|---|---|---|---|
| | Firms X and Y | Firm X—Purchase | Firm Y—Lease |
| Assets | $200 | $300 | $200 |
| Total | $200 | $300 | $200 |
| Debt | $100 | $200 | $100 |
| Equity | 100 | 100 | 100 |
| Total | $200 | $300 | $200 |

Both firms have debt to equity ratios of 50 percent before the purchase.

The companies decide to acquire assets of $100,000. Firm X decides to borrow $100,000; thus an asset and a liability enter its balance sheet, and its debt to equity ratio increases to 75 percent. Firm Y leases the equipment. The lease may call for fixed charges as high as, or even higher than, the loan, but the fact that the debt to equity ratio of Firm Y remains the same as before the lease (50 percent) might enable Firm Y to borrow money when Firm X, because of its higher debt to equity ratio, could not.

## Financial Accounting Standards Board Statement on Accounting for Leases (FASB No. 13)

Financial Accounting Standards Board Statement No. 13 specifies how to account for leases. This statement supersedes Accounting Principles Board (APB) Opinions 5, 7, 27, 31 and paragraph 15 of APB Opinion No. 18.

FASB No. 13 divides leases (from the lessee's standpoint) into two groups: (1) capital leases, which are considered purchases of assets, and (2) operating leases, which are all other leases.

*Capital Leases* If at its inception a lease meets one or more of the following four criteria, the lease is classified as a capital lease. The criteria are:

1 The lease transfers ownership of the property to the lessee by the end of the lease term.

2 The lease contains a bargain purchase option (a provision allowing the lessee, at his option, to purchase the leased property for a price that is lower than the expected fair market value of the property on the option date).

3 The lease term is equal to 75 percent or more of the estimated economic life of the leased property. However, if the beginning of the lease term falls within the last 25 percent of the total estimated economic life of the leased

property, including earlier years of use, this criterion shall not be used for purposes of classifying the lease.

4   The present value at the beginning of the lease term of the minimum lease payments, excluding that portion of the payments representing executory costs (costs paid by the lessor), equals or exceeds 90 percent of the excess of the fair market value of the leased property to the lessor above any investment tax credit retained by the lessor. However, if the beginning of the lease term falls within the last 25 percent of the total estimated economic life of the leased property, this criterion shall not be used for purposes of classifying a lease.

A capital lease is recorded as an asset and a lease obligation (liability) equal to the present value of the lease payments during the term of the lease. The present value calculation would exclude such costs as insurance, maintenance, and taxes to be paid by the lessor. If this present value exceeds the fair market value of the leased property at the beginning of the lease period, the capitalized lease asset is recorded at fair market value.

The capital lease is amortized (depreciated) as follows. If the capital lease meets criterion 1 or 2, mentioned above, the asset can be amortized in a manner consistent with the lessee's normal depreciation policy for owned assets. If the lease does not meet criterion 1 or 2, but meets criterion 3 or 4, the leased asset is amortized in the normal manner except that the period of amortization is the term of the lease.

During the term of the capital lease, each lease payment is allocated between a reduction in the lease obligation and interest expense in a manner similar to the repayment of an installment loan or mortgage.

Assets recorded under capital leases and the amortization of such assets must be separately identified in the lessee's balance sheet and the footnotes to the balance sheet.

*Capital leases* require the following disclosures:

1   The gross amount of the capital leases bv nature or function.

2   Future lease payments as of the date of the balance sheet and in aggregate for each of the five succeeding years. Separate deductions representing executory costs (costs paid by lessor) and the amount of imputed interest necessary to reduce the lease payments to present value must also be included.

3   The total amount of sublease rentals to be received in the future under noncancelable subleases.

4   Total contingent rentals (rentals dependent on some factor other than the passage of time) incurred in each period for which there is an income statement.

*Operating leases* require the following disclosures:

1 Future rental payments required as of the date of the balance sheet and in aggregate for each of the 5 succeeding fiscal years.
2 The total rentals to be received in the future under noncancelable subleases.
3 Restrictions imposed by lease agreements, such as those concerning dividends, additional debt, and further leasing.

FASB No. 13 also contains specific recommendations with regard to direct financing leases, sale-leasebacks, leveraged leases, and land and building leases. These matters will be discussed in later chapters.

FASB No. 13 has been amended and interpreted a number of times by the FASB. FASB Statement Nos. 17, 22, 23, 26, 27, 28, and 29 contain amendments to Statement No. 13. FASB Interpretation Nos. 19, 21, 23, 24, 26, and 27 contain interpretations of FASB No. 13. In addition, certain FASB Staff Technical Bulletins interpret FASB No. 13. In May 1980, the FASB issued an updated version of FASB No. 13 that incorporates all amendments and interpretations of the Statement to that date. We recommend that the reader obtain a copy of the updated version of FASB No. 13 as a companion to this volume.

# Chapter 2

# ACCOUNTING ASPECTS OF LEASE FINANCING

Until the issuance of FASB No. 13, four Accounting Principles Board Opinions (APB Nos. 5, 7, 27, and 31) dealt with accounting for leases. These opinions generated debate because they did not provide symmetrical accounting treatment between the parties to lease arrangements. Therefore, when the Financial Accounting Standards Board came into existence in 1973, the subject of accounting for leases was one of its original agenda items.

This chapter will discuss accounting for leases under FASB No. 13 and its various amendments and interpretations. It will also provide some analysis of the major issues addressed in FASB No. 13. Specific emphasis will be directed at the classification of leases and the accounting and reporting treatment applied to various leasing arrangements.

The following points summarize the significant aspects of accounting for leases that have resulted from the issuance of FASB No. 13:

1  Symmetrical accounting for lessors and lessees since the criteria used in determining whether a lease should be capitalized are essentially the same for both parties.

2  Segregation of the capitalized leased asset and the related capitalized lease obligation is required for balance sheet purposes.

3  Lessors, including manufacturer/dealer lessors, can recognize profit on sales-type leases.

4  Disclosure requirements are expanded.

5  Leases involving various categories of real estate have been identified, with the criteria for capitalization outlined for each category.

6  Extensive coverage of leveraged leases.

7  Expansion of the coverage of related party leases.

8  The accounts of subsidiaries whose principal business activity is leasing

property or facilities to the parent or other affiliated companies must be consolidated.

In an attempt to provide guidance for compliance with the requirements of FASB No. 13, some aids have been developed. These include:

1   An official summary of FASB No. 13 prepared by the FASB.
2   A list of amendments, interpretations, and staff technical bulletins dealing with FASB No. 13.
3   Flow charts of accounting for leases prepared by the FASB.

**"Official Summary of FASB No. 13"**

FASB Statement No. 13, *Accounting for Leases,* and its various amendments and interpretations (all of which have been incorporated into this publication) specify the classification, accounting, and reporting of leases by lessors and lessees. The provisions of that Statement derive from the view that a lease that transfers substantially all of the benefits and risks of ownership should be accounted for as the acquisition of an asset and the incurrence of an obligation by the lessee (a capital lease) and as a sale or financing by the lessor (a sales-type, direct financing, or leveraged lease). Other leases should be accounted for as operating leases, that is, the rental of property.

Required disclosures of lessees and lessors are specified and special guidance is provided for various matters including leveraged leases, leases involving real estate, leases involving related parties, subleases, the effect of business combinations on the classification of leases, and sale-leaseback transactions.

The provisions are generally effective for leasing transactions and lease agreement revisions entered into on or after January 1, 1977, although some revised provisions became effective later. Retroactive application to all leases, regardless of when they were entered into, is generally required in financial statements for calendar or fiscal years beginning after December 31, 1980.

A lessee classifies a lease as either a capital lease or an operating lease. If a particular lease meets any one of the following classification criteria, it is a capital lease:

a.   The lease transfers ownership of the property to the lessee by the end of the lease term.

b.   The lease contains an option to purchase the leased property at a bargain price.

c.   The lease term is equal to or greater than 75 percent of the estimated economic life of the leased property.

d.  The present value of rental and other minimum lease payments equals or exceeds 90 percent of the fair value of the leased property less any investment tax credit retained by the lessor.

The last two criteria are not applicable when the beginning of the lease term falls within the last 25 percent of the total estimated economic life of the leased property. The amount to be recorded by the lessee as an asset and an obligation under a capital lease is the lesser of the present value of the rental and other minimum lease payments or the fair value of the leased property. Leased property under a capital lease is amortized in a manner consistent with the lessee's normal depreciation policy for owned assets; the amortization period is restricted to the lease term, rather than the life of the asset, unless the lease provides for transfer of title or includes a bargain purchase option. The periodic rental payments are treated as payments of the lease obligation and as interest expense (principal and interest) so that a constant periodic rate of interest is recorded on the remaining balance of the obligation.

If none of the criteria is met, the lease is classified as an operating lease by a lessee. Neither an asset nor an obligation is recorded for operating leases. Rental payments are recorded as rental expense in the income statement in a systematic manner, which is usually straight-line.

From the lessor's perspective, a lease is classified as a sales-type, direct financing, leveraged, or operating lease. To be classified as a sales-type, direct financing, or leveraged lease, a lease must meet one of the four classification criteria specified above and *both* of the following two further criteria:

a.  Collectibility of the minimum lease payments is reasonably predictable.
b.  No important uncertainties surround the amount of unreimbursable costs yet to be incurred by the lessor under the lease.

A lease meeting those criteria is classified as a sales-type lease if the fair value of the leased property is different from its carrying amount. Otherwise, unless the lease meets certain additional criteria for leveraged leases, a lease meeting one of the first four criteria and both of the last two is classified as a direct financing lease. There are further criteria for classification as a sales-type lease when the leased property is real estate. Leases that fail to meet the foregoing criteria are classified as operating leases.

For a sales-type lease, the present value of the minimum lease payments receivable from the lessee is reported as sales and the carrying amount of the leased property plus any initial direct costs, less the present value of any unguaranteed residual value, is charged as cost of sales. The lessor reports as an asset on the balance sheet the net investment in a sales-type lease calculated by recording the gross investment (the sum of the minimum lease payments and the unguaranteed residual value) at its present value, using the interest rate implicit in the lease as the discount factor. The difference between the gross investment and the net investment is

FASB STATEMENT NO. 13 AS AMENDED AND INTERPRETED THROUGH MAY 1980 (Stamford, Conn.: FASB, 1980), pp. iii–xiii. © Financial Accounting Standards Board. Reprinted with permission. Copies of the complete document may be obtained from the FASB.

unearned income, which is amortized over the lease term so as to produce a constant periodic rate of return on the net investment.

For a lease classified as a direct financing lease, the lessor reports as an asset on the balance sheet the net investment in a lease consisting of gross investment less unearned income. The gross investment is calculated in the same way as for a sales-type lease (the sum of the minimum lease payments and the unguaranteed residual value). Unearned income is determined by subtracting the cost or carrying amount of the leased property from the gross investment. Unearned income is amortized over the lease term so as to produce a constant periodic rate of return on the net investment.

A leveraged lease is a direct financing lease that additionally has all of the following characteristics:

a.   It involves at least three parties: a lessee, a long-term creditor, and a lessor.
b.   The financing provided by the long-term creditor is substantial to the transaction and is nonrecourse to the lessor.
c.   The lessor's net investment declines during the early years and increases during the later years of the lease term.
d.   Any investment tax credit retained by the lessor is accounted for as one of the cash flow components of the lease.

The lessor records the investment in a leveraged lease net of the nonrecourse debt. Income is recognized only in periods in which the net investment net of related deferred taxes is positive. The total net income over the lease term is calculated by deducting the original investment from total cash receipts. By using projected cash receipts and disbursements, the rate of return on the net investment in the years in which the investment is positive is determined and applied to the net investment to determine the periodic income to be recognized. The assumption that underlies this accounting is that the lessor will earn other income during the years in which the investment is negative (net funds are provided by the lease) and will not expect the lease to provide income during those years.

A lessor accounts for leases not meeting the criteria for classification as sales-type, direct financing, or leveraged leases as operating leases. Leased property under operating leases is recorded in the same way as other property, plant, and equipment; rent is reported as income over the lease term in a systematic manner which is usually straight-line; and the leased property is depreciated like other productive assets.

Leases involving real estate are also addressed. Briefly, if the leased property is land only, the lease is classified as an operating lease unless it provides for transfer of title or includes a bargain purchase option. If the leased property is land and buildings, this document specifies whether and how the elements are to be separated and which criteria are to be applied. Leases that cover only part of a building are addressed and guidance is provided in determining whether the fair value of that part of a building can be determined objectively.

FASB STATEMENT NO. 13 AS AMENDED AND INTERPRETED THROUGH MAY 1980 (Stamford, Conn.: FASB, 1980), pp. iii–xiii. © Financial Accounting Standards Board. Reprinted with permission. Copies of the complete document may be obtained from the FASB.

\*     \*     \*     \*     \*

Certain provisions of this document are summarized visually in the following decision trees. [The key for the decision trees follows:]

| Abbreviation | Short for |
| --- | --- |
| Acc. | Account |
| BPO | Bargain Purchase Option |
| BRO | Bargain Renewal Option |
| Coll. | Collectibility |
| Conting. | Contingency |
| Disc. | Discounted |
| ELife | Economic Life |
| FV | Fair Value |
| Guar. | Guarantee |
| Incr. BRate | Incremental Borrowing Rate |
| Imp. IRate | Implicit Interest Rate |
| Int. | Interest |
| Inv. | Investment |
| ITC | Investment Tax Credit |
| Liab. | Liability |
| LP | Leased Property |
| LT | Lease Term |
| L-T | Long-Term |
| MLP | Minimum Lease Payments |
| MRP | Minimum Rental Payments |
| Nonrec. | Nonrecourse |
| Oblig. | Obligation |
| Orig. | Original |
| Own. | Ownership |
| P/L | Profit or Loss |
| Purch. | Purchase |
| R | Renewal |
| Reas. | Reasonably |
| Rec. | Recognition |
| Req. | Require |
| Reqs. | Requirements |
| RV | Residual Value |
| Tsfr. | Transfer |
| Unreimb. | Unreimbursable |

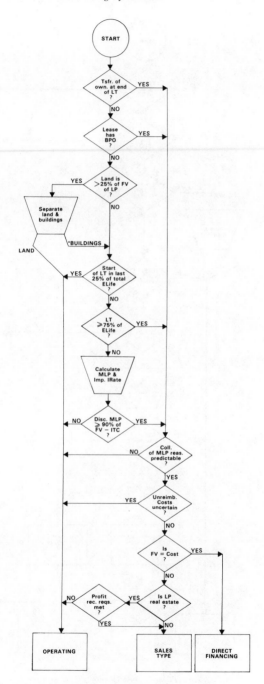

*This document also addresses part of a building.

FASB STATEMENT NO. 13 AS AMENDED AND INTERPRETED THROUGH MAY 1980 (Stamford, Conn.: FASB, 1980), pp. iii–xiii. © Financial Accounting Standards Board. Reprinted with permission. Copies of the complete document may be obtained from the FASB.

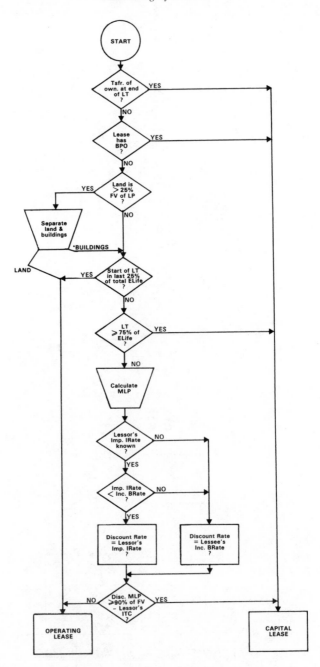

*This document also addresses part of a building.

FASB STATEMENT NO. 13 AS AMENDED AND INTERPRETED THROUGH MAY 1980 (Stamford, Conn.: FASB, 1980), pp. iii–xiii. © Financial Accounting Standards Board. Reprinted with permission. Copies of the complete document may be obtained from the FASB.

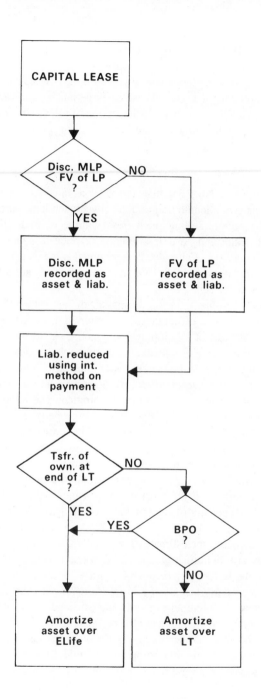

## ISSUES RELATED TO ACCOUNTING FOR LEASES

FASB No. 13, requires the lessee and lessor to utilize similar accounting rules to classify and account for leases. These rules pertain to fair value, economic life, and residual value. Following is a discussion of rules and some of the ways the rules are being applied to accounting for leases in practice.

### Fair Value

Paragraph 5(c) of FASB No. 13 defines fair value as the price for which property could be sold in an arm's-length transaction between unrelated parties. Fair value is defined as the normal selling price (less volume or trade discounts) of a manufacturer or dealer and cost (less volume or trade discounts) for the non-manufacturer or nondealer. Fair value is determined at the inception of the lease. FASB No. 13 refers only to the fair value of the property, not to the fair value of the lease or property rights.

There are many problems in the estimation of fair value. Real property is the source of most of these difficulties. Paragraph 28 of FASB No. 13 refers to leases covering only part of a building. Paragraph 28 states that unless the fair value of the leased property is objectively determinable, the lessee shall classify the lease according to the 75 percent economic life test. Some have taken this to mean that if the fair value is difficult to determine for any leased property, the 90 percent test of paragraph 7(d) may be omitted. The FASB believes that difficulty in determining the fair value of leased property does not justify the omission of its use. FASB Interpretation No. 24, Leases Involving Only Part of a Building, provides guidance in this area and suggests that appraisal or replacement cost information may indicate fair value.

Fair value is used in many areas of lease accounting. Its most prominent use is in the test to determine if the present value of the minimum lease payments meets or exceeds 90 percent of the fair value of the leased property (paragraph 7d of FASB No. 13). Fair value plays a role in the calculation of the interest rate implicit in the lease, the estimate of residual value, bargain renewal option, and bargain purchase option. In addition, fair value becomes an upper limit on the amount that the lessee may record as an asset for a capital lease.

The age of a property has an impact on estimating its fair value. Difficulty may be encountered in obtaining records and information on old property. Inflation and technological change can also be factors.

For recently acquired property, cost is usually a reasonable measure of fair value. The fair value of new real property to a builder/lessor or to a developer/lessor ordinarily will be its normal selling price. If a developer sells property to an investor, the investor's cost would be the developer's normal selling price. The fair value of new real property to an investor/lessor will ordinarily be its cost. If the land on which the property was developed was held for a period, the value of the land may have increased due to factors other than the development. Changes in the value of land should be considered for the period between its acquisition by the developer and the inception of the lease. If the fair value of the land is 25 percent or more of the total fair value of the leased property at the inception of the lease, then the land and building must be considered separately for purposes of applying the lease classification criteria.

Determining fair value at the inception of the lease for used property involves the retrieval of information that may be lost or that may never have existed. It means looking back to the date of inception of the lease and ignoring conditions that have developed since that time. The lessee and lessor must form their judgments as to the classification of a lease on the basis of conditions existing at the inception of the lease.

As noted previously, FASB No. 13 recognizes that the fair value of a part of a building may not be objectively determinable. If the fair value cannot be objectively determined, the lessee will classify the lease as an operating lease. (It should be noted that the concept of "objectively determined" is applicable only to leases involving part of a building. In all other cases, FASB No. 13 does not provide an exemption from the requirement to determine fair value. FASB Interpretation No. 24 states that other evidence may provide a basis for objective determination of fair value even if there are no sales of property similar to the leased property.)

The fair value of a part of a whole cannot be objectively determined in many instances. The part of a whole problem is most common in leases involving part of shopping centers, regional malls, office buildings, or warehouses. The determination that the leased property is part of a whole is not always straightforward. A floor in a multistory office building is part of a whole. A shop occupying a small portion of a shopping center is part of a whole. A store that is not an integral part of the structure of a shopping center probably is not a part of a whole. The following are some characteristics that may identify property that is not part of a whole:

1  Freestanding structure.
2  Separate financing.
3  Separate entity for property tax purposes.
4  Facilities that are separable, that is, facilities that are independent in terms of utilities, maintenance, and other similar factors.

Many shopping centers or regional malls contain one or more stores that, because of their relative size or drawing power, would be considered to be the dominant store or stores. Even though the dominant store or stores may be considered to be a part of a whole, the fair value of such stores may be objectively determinable because of their dominant position in the shopping center.

FASB No. 13 does not provide any basis for concluding that a freestanding structure can be considered to be a part of a whole. In most instances a free-standing structure is an entity for which fair value must be determined.

Fair value may be considered to have been objectively determined if the lessee follows a reasonable, acceptable, and consistent approach and if there is no indication that the fair value has been prejudiced. The lessee does not have to prove that the fair value is correct; the lessee has to show it is appropriate to use in accounting for leases.

Most of the fair value problems encountered are on the lessee side of the leasing transaction. The following are some of the ways the lessee may be able to estimate the fair value:

1   Ask the lessor to furnish data suitable for estimating fair value. This might be in the form of lessor cost data or an unexercised option to purchase the property.

2   Request loan-to-value ratio information. This method results in a rough ap-proximation that may not be suitable in cases where a more precise value is needed.

3   Search files and records for economic studies that may have been made at or near the inception of the lease. The valuation data in such studies may be difficult to corroborate, but it could lend support to other data.

4   Obtain valuation data for the assessment of property or ad valorem taxes. Valuations for tax purposes may or may not bear a known relationship to the fair value of the property. The relationship should be ascertained prior to using the assessment data.

5   Consider using replacement cost data that may have been developed in com-pliance with Accounting Series Release No. 190 or FASB Statement No. 33. If a good faith effort was made in the estimation of replacement cost data, this data could be discounted back to the inception date of the lease. The discounting would be accomplished by using an appropriate index.

Valuation specialists have developed formal methods to estimate the fair value of various kinds of property. The methods differ depending on whether the property is real or tangible personal property. These methods were developed for valuations used in mergers, acquisitions, and property tax situations.

***Real Property***   For real property, the lessee may follow one of the following generally recognized methods: the cost approach, the market data approach, or the income approach. The cost approach involves calculating the estimated re-production cost of the facility and its improvements, less depreciation, plus the estimated value of the land if it were vacant. The market data or comparative sales approach compares the property to be valued with recent sales of similar property in the same geographical location within a particular period. The income approach involves capitalizing net income from the property to be valued by applying a rate representing the relationship between the property and the net income it should be capable of producing. This approach or a variation of this approach is the most commonly used method to value real property. Caution must be exercised when using this approach, because the terms of the lease should not be used to value the property. The net income from a given property may or may not be equal to what it is under the terms of the lease. The net income from the property would be what an unrelated third party or parties would be willing to pay over the entire economic life of the property.

*Machinery and Equipment*  For machinery and equipment, the lessee may estimate fair value through direct pricing or indexing. Direct pricing refers to construction costs or purchase prices found in catalogs, vendor quotations, or engineering estimates. Indexing refers to the application of the appropriate indices to the historical cost of the equipment. The lessee may estimate the value of furniture and fixtures by either the comparison method or the price guide method. The comparison method involves determining the selling price for such property adjusted for the trend of current prices. The price guide method requires the classification of the property in terms of its condition and the application of a standard price guide.

The process of determining the fair value of leased property is one of estimation and not one of precision. The degree of precision desired should be based on the materiality of the leases and the potential result of an error in classification or misuse of valuation data. The lessee and lessor should use a reasonable approach to estimating fair value that can be applied consistently from situation to situation.

## Economic Life

The economic life of leased property is defined in FASB No. 13 as the estimated remaining period during which the property is expected to be economically usable by one or more users, with normal repairs and maintenance, for the purpose for which it was intended at the inception of the lease, without limitation by the lease term.

The definition in FASB No. 13 does not differ significantly from that used for APB Opinion No. 27, Accounting For Lease Transactions by Manufacturer or Dealer Lessors. In addition, the economic lives used for ASR No. 147 generally complied with the definition in APB Opinion No. 27. Therefore, the economic life concept under FASB No. 13 should not, in most circumstances, involve significant changes in previously determined economic lives. However, the economic life in each leasing situation should be reviewed by the lessee or lessor to be sure that FASB No. 13 is applicable.

The estimation of the economic life of leased property is important primarily because it is one of the criteria used to classify the lease. In addition, economic life has a bearing on residual value.

The difficulties in estimating economic life are not significantly different from those encountered in establishing depreciable lives. Whether property is owned or rented should not affect the estimate of economic life. Depreciation is defined in accounting as the allocation of cost of an asset over the estimated useful life of an asset. Useful life and economic life appear to be substantially the same. Therefore, depreciable lives may be a sound basis on which to estimate economic lives for comparable assets.

In the retail industry, there has been considerable discussion of economic lives. One of the main topics has been shopping centers and the theory put forth by some that the economic lives of shopping centers are considerably longer than their depreciable lives. Several studies and other sources have been brought forward to substantiate the various economic life estimates. However, the studies generally show that economic lives coincide with depreciable lives. As with any guidelines, these sources are based on averages and contain certain assumptions. The circumstances vary from situation to situation and each instance may be modified by experience or knowledge of circumstances differing from the assumptions. One example of an authoritative source is the Gladstone Associates study entitled *Shopping Center Useful Lives: An Economic Analysis.*

The following are examples of typical average economic lives:

| | |
|---|---|
| Shopping centers | |
| Mall | 40 years |
| Strip | 30 years |
| Freestanding buildings | |
| Single floor | 33 years* |
| Multiple floors | 45 years |
| Warehouses | 35–40 years |

The economic life of leased property is limited by the use for which it was intended at the inception of the lease. The number of users is not a factor as long as they continue to use the property as intended.

---

*Special purpose facilities may have lives considerably shorter than 33 years. For instance, some food stores have been constructed in such a way as to indicate a 20–25 year life as being more appropriate.

The intended use of a property is subject to interpretation. A significant change in the use of a property would shorten the economic life estimate. One way of measuring the significance of a change would be if property required more than nominal modifications to accommodate the new purpose or use. For example, converting a retail store into a warehouse or making a retail store into an office would appear to be significant changes. Changing a retail store into a discount store would not appear to be significant.

## Residual Value

FASB No. 13 defines the residual value of leased property as the estimated fair value of the property at the end of the lease term. In other words, residual value involves the determination of fair value at the end of the lease. The added complication is the unpredictability of future events.

Residual value has accounting significance for both the lessee and the lessor. In determining the present value of minimum lease payments, the lessee must discount the stream of payments by the lower of an incremental borrowing rate or the interest rate implicit in the lease. Usually the lessee cannot determine the lessor's implicit interest rate, and an estimate must be made, if it is obvious that the implicit interest rate is less than the incremental borrowing rate and that the incremental borrowing rate would not cause capitalization. The residual value accruing to the benefit of the lessor is a factor included in the estimate of the implicit rate.

The residual value is of importance to the lessor, because the lessor records as part of its gross investment in the lease the estimated residual value accruing to its benefit.

The residual value concept is not new. A property owner has estimated salvage value for depreciation purposes. Since salvage values tend to be conservative and tax-oriented, methods used for estimating salvage value may or may not be appropriate for residual value estimation.

The lessor or lessee may have past experience with similar leased properties. The relationship of residual value to cost or fair value in the past may be a reasonable guide for making a current estimate.

In some circumstances, it may be appropriate to estimate the residual value by applying a ratio of the economic life remaining at the end of the lease term to the total economic life times the estimated fair value at the inception of the lease. This method should be used with caution since it assumes a straight-line relationship between the passage of time and the decrease of fair value. Prices charged by dealers for used property may be useful where such situations can be identified. The lessee or lessor mav seek an appraiser's opinion as to the residual value.

FASB No. 13, as written, was silent on the topic of inflation. As a consequence, whether inflation should or should not be included in making estimates of residual values is unresolved. In May 1979 the FASB issued an exposure draft of an amendment to FASB No. 13 that would have specified that inflation should not be considered when making estimates of residual values. However, this exposure draft was withdrawn in November 1979 as a result of adverse criticism.

## EXAMPLES OF THE APPLICATION OF FASB 13 TO LEASE TRANSACTIONS

**Example 1** State public utility commissions usually exclude leased assets from the rate base of the public utility. Are utilities exempt from the lease capitalization requirements of FASB No. 13 because of the provisions of the Addendum to APB Opinion No. 2 that allows rate regulated utilities to use public utility commission accounting? The answer is yes, providing that the appropriate regulatory authorities do not recognize capital leases for rate-making purposes. At this time there is some disagreement as to how FASB No. 13 should be applied to rate regulated utilities. The primary point of contention is whether or not the Addendum to APB No. 2 relates only to the income statement or encompasses both the income statement and balance sheet. Treating a transaction differently in the same financial statements (i.e., as an operating lease for income statement purposes and as a capital lease for balance sheet purposes) is both inconsistent and illogical. The classification of leases affects the timing of income recognition and, as such, should probably be under the Addendum. Even if capitalized, the resulting asset would not be included in the utility rate base. Accordingly, lease capitalization or balance sheet and income statement "as if" disclosures in those circumstances would not seem to be appropriate.

However, the SEC has included a provision in Accounting Series Release No. 225 that requires a utility to disclose the aggregate amounts of assets and liabilities for each required balance sheet and the effect on net income for each required income statement for leases that meet the definition of a capital lease under FASB No. 13 but are accounted for as operating leases. The SEC has requested that the FASB reconsider or interpret the Addendum. Until such time, the SEC will require the "as if" disclosures. The FASB has issued a discussion memorandum dealing with accounting for rate regulated industries. It is possible that the FASB may interpret the Addendum to require either lease capitalization or "as if" disclosure.

**Example 2** A December 31 year-end company signs a lease on November 1. The term of the lease and usage of the leased property are expected to begin the following February. The lessor is in possession of the property, which is ready for use by the lessee any time after November 1. Assuming that the lease qualifies as a capital lease, should the lease be recorded as of November 1, the date of the lease agreement, or February 1, the beginning of the lease term?

Paragraph 10 of FASB No. 13 states that the lessee shall record a capital lease as an obligation at an amount equal to the present value at the beginning of the lease term of minimum lease payments. This means that the asset and obligation will be recorded as of the beginning of the lease term, February 1 in the example.

The FASB has issued FASB Statement No. 23, an amendment to FASB No. 13, defining the inception of the lease as the date of the lease agreement. This requires the measurement of amounts as of the agreement date, but should not cause such amounts to be recorded prior to the commencement of the lease term.

**Example 3**  A lessor establishes rent such that the present value of the minimum lease payments equal 89 percent of the excess of the fair value of the leased property to the lessor at the inception of the lease over any related Investment Tax Credit retained and expected to be realized. In addition, the lessor requires the lessee to pay a deposit that is fully refundable at the end of the lease term. Any earnings on the deposit belong to the lessor; no interest is paid to the lessee. Should the deposit and the interest earned thereon be included in minimum lease payments for the 90 percent test?

The time-value of money should be considered as part of the rent because it involves a cost to the lessee and a benefit to the lessor.

Paragraph 5(j) (i) states that payments the lessee is obligated to make are included in minimum lease payments. The lessee is required to make the deposit, but it is refunded in full at the end of the lease term. The deposit should be included in the minimum lease payments as of the date paid and the amount of the rent payments at the end of the lease should be reduced by equal amount.

**Example 4**  Paragraph 7(b) stipulates that a lessee should classify a lease as a capital lease if it contains a bargain purchase option. Paragraph 5(d) defines a bargain purchase option as an option to purchase the leased property for a price that is sufficiently lower than the expected fair value of the property at the date the option becomes exercisable that exercise of the option appears, at the inception of the lease, to be reasonably assured. Are there factors other than the expected fair value of the leased property that should be considered in making such a determination?

The underlying basis of the bargain purchase test is whether or not exercise of the option is reasonably assured. Measurement of the fair value of property at the end of a long-term lease is at best a subjective measurement. An indication of reasonable assurance may be obtained from a review of the expected value of lease-hold improvements at the end of the lease. Substantial remaining undepreciated cost in these improvements may be supportive of renewal of the lease, while little or no remaining value in these improvements may be indicative of an intent to let the lease expire.

**Example 5** FASB No. 13 defines the lease term as including all periods, if any, covered by ordinary renewal options preceding the date at which a bargain purchase option becomes exercisable. A lease for equipment may have an initial term of 10 years with an option to renew for a second 10 years at the same price, with an option to purchase the equipment for $1 at the end of the renewal period. There is a clear expectation that the value of the equipment 20 years hence will be significantly greater than $1. However, it is not at all clear that the utility of the equipment during the second 10 year period will be sufficient to warrant exercising the renewal option, despite the existence of the option to buy for a dollar. Does this situation indicate that the lease term is 10 years or 20 years?

Based on the facts as stated, the lease term is probably 10 years and the bargain purchase option would be disregarded. Exercise of the purchase option is reasonably assured, but only if the renewal option is first exercised. In the absence of a use for the equipment to the lessee during the second 10 years, the renewal option would be exercised only in the event that the present value of the expected residual value of the equipment at the end of 20 years exceeds the present value of the lease payments during the renewal period.

**Example 6** Many leases require payments based on something other than the passage of time. Leases for shopping center stores often provide for rents based on a percentage of sales. Some leases are tied to interest rates. How are contingent rentals based on formulas treated in determining the classification of leases?

The general rule is that contingent rentals should not be included in the determination of minimum lease payments. In some cases the contingency may be so remote as to be nonexistent for all practical purposes. In such circumstances, the rent should not be viewed as contingent and should be included in the minimum lease payments. Some examples of this distinction between contingent and noncontingent are:

1   A 15 year lease calls for rentals of $50,000 per year beginning in year three. For years one and two, the annual rent is to be the product of $500,000 times the prime interest rate. Since the amount of rent for the first two years will vary with changes in the prime interest rate, there are those who would argue that the entire rental for those years should be disregarded. This is probably an incorrect interpretation. There will be a prime interest rate; therefore, there will be come amount of rental. Neither the lessor nor the lessee can influence the rate; therefore, some reasonable estimate of the amount payable must be included in the calculation of minimum lease payments. If the present prime rate was 10 percent and, based on reasonable investigation, if the

likelihood of the prime rate falling to 8 percent is reasonable, but the like-lihood of a rate below 8 percent is remote, then 8 percent should be used to calculate the first 2 years' rent.

2  A lease on a retail store site calls for annual rental of 1000 percent of the first $25,000 annual sales. Attainment of that sales level is virtually certain as long as the store stays open. There are, however, no legal or contractual requirements for the company to keep the store open. Because the lessee can influence the amount of the rent, in this case the rent is contingent and should not be included. In June 1979, the FASB issued an amendment to FASB No. 13 dealing with the determination of contingent rentals. The Amendment focused on the measurement of the contingent rental rather than on the probability of the contingency taking effect.

**Example 7**   So-called standard funding disclaimer clauses are common in leases negotiated by state and local government units. Funding disclaimer clauses provide that an agreement is cancelable if the legislature or other governing body fails to appropriate funds for future payments. Can such clauses be considered to be remote contingencies within the provisions of paragraph 5(f), thus rendering the lease noncancelable within the definition of paragraph 5(f) and allowing treatment as a capital lease?

Standard funding disclaimer clauses do constitute real and substantive can-cellation rights; however, such clauses are infrequently exercised. Consequently, leases containing such clauses may be considered as noncancelable based on the judgment that the probability of cancellation is remote.

Factors to be considered in arriving at a judgment regarding the probability of cancellation include: the history of the lessor with respect to similar leases; the fiscal status of the lessee; whether the lease is treated as a capital lease by the lessee; whether the leased asset is essential to continued normal operation of the governmental unit; legal opinions as to noncancelability. See FASB Staff Technical Bulletin No. 79-10, Fiscal Funding Clauses in Lease Agreements, for further discussion.

**Example 8**   A company has established an estimated asset lives policy for property that it has purchased or leased. The asset lives were determined for purposes of book and tax depreciation and for purposes of FASB No. 30 on current cost disclosure. May a company establish estimated economic lives for purposes of applying FASB No. 13 that differ significantly from those asset lives established as noted above?

Estimated economic lives established for the application of FASB No. 13 should not be inconsistent with asset lives established for other accounting ap-plications that require useful life determinations. Asset lives established for other purposes create a presumption that one or the other of the useful life estimates is in error.

**Example 9**    Insurance has been available from Lloyds of London that provides payment to the lessor for certain payments that the lessee would otherwise have been obligated to make on cancellation of (or failure to renew) a lease. Should such payment be considered the same as a payment to be received directly from a lessee in determining minimum lease payments from the standpoint of the lessor?

If the insurance policy is such that it guarantees the residual value of the leased property or rental payments beyond the lease term, such a guarantee would be included in minimum lease payments by the lessor.

Each insurance policy should be reviewed to ascertain if it is truly a third-party guarantee of lease payments or of residual value. Most of the policies are written to indemnify the lessor for its liability to repay debt related to the acquisition of leased equipment "solely and directly in consequence of the termination of or nonrenewal of any declared lease agreement."

The following are examples of insurance provisions that should not be regarded as guarantees of lease payments or residual value: the insurance policy contains limitations with respect to the relationship between the purchase price of the equipment and the insured debt (e.g., debt cannot exceed 83 percent of the purchase price); it excludes losses due to insolvency of the lessee or equipment manufacturer; it requires the establishment of equipment pools, surplus revenue from which will provide insurance up to the level of any claim; it provides the insurer with "any sum occurring from the sale or release of equipment upon the termination or nonrenewal of the lease not to exceed the amount of claims paid."

**Example 10**    Certain types of transportation equipment may be subsidized by a governmental agency. The subsidy may be returned by the lessor to the lessee in the form of a rent credit. Should rent credits based on factors other than the passage of time be included in minimum lease payments for the recovery of investment test [paragraph 7(d)]?

If rent credits are contingent on something other than the passage of time, they should be excluded from minimum lease payments. This is consistent with the exclusion of contingent rent expense from minimum lease payments.

**Example 11**    Minimum lease payments, as defined in paragraphs 5(j) and 7(d), exclude executory costs. What constitutes executory costs for this purpose and how should such costs be estimated?

Executory costs are those incurred by the lessor in connection with owning and operating the property, such as repairs, maintenance, insurance, and property taxes. Estimates of executory costs should be based on the lessor's experience with similar property, the advice of experts, or reference to tax rate structures.

Estimates of executory costs should consider the behavior of such costs over time. For example, repairs and maintenance would be expected to rise over time. Note the profit on executory costs is also to be considered.

**Example 12**   A company is lessee of many pieces of similar equipment obtained from one lessor. The lessor has given the company a letter stating "Please be advised that while we do not provide accounting advice, we treat all existing leases, including those on which you are the lessee, as operating leases for our own internal accounting purposes. This lease classification has been reviewed with our independent accountants who concur with our classification." Recognizing the concept of symmetry in FASB No. 13, would such a letter be sufficient to allow classification of these leases as operating leases?

Reliance should not be placed on such a letter; management must make its own determination based on a review and analysis of the leases.

**Example 13**   The following practice is used in the computer leasing industry. A 5 year noncancelable lease is entered into between an equipment lessor and lessee (in many cases using a broker as an intermediary). Under a separate agreement (side agreement) the broker, or in some cases the lessor, undertakes to reimburse the lessee for rental payments required in the fourth and fifth years of the lease, providing that the equipment is made available to the broker (or lessor, if appropriate) for remarketing. How should lessees and lessors account for this form of transaction?

*Lessee*   The side agreement, whether between the broker and lessee or the lessor and lessee, does not relieve the lessee of its primary obligation under the lease, except to the extent that the lessor (and any party that has rights arising from the lessor) explicitly releases the lessee from obligation. As such, the side agreement should be viewed as a contingent sublease to be accounted for as follows:

1   A noncancelable term of 5 years should be used in accounting for the lease as the lease is independent of the side agreement.
2   If the side agreement is implemented, the accounting prescribed in paragraph 39 of FASB No. 13 (subleases) should be applied. That is, the original lessee should continue to account for the obligation related to the original lease as before. The side agreement should be accounted for as a sublease in accordance with paragraphs 39(a), 39(b), or 39(c), as appropriate.

The amount paid for the side agreement should be excluded from minimum lease payments.

*Lessor*   When the side agreement is between the broker and the lessee, the lessor's accounting is not affected by the side agreement. However, in those cases where the side agreement is between the lessor and lessee, the lease generally is accounted for on the basis of the shorter lease term (for which no reimbursement is available), which will generally result in an operating lease. The obligation imposed by the side agreement usually constitutes an important uncertainty surrounding the amount of unreimbursable costs yet to be incurred under the lease. Accordingly, the lease does not meet the criteria of paragraph 8b required for sales-type or direct financing lease classification. Reference should be made to FASB Interpretation No. 19.

**Example 14**   The lessee and lessor agree to make retroactive changes in the provisions of an existing lease by means other than renewing the lease or extending its term. Such changes would have resulted in a different classification of the lease under the criteria of paragraphs 7 and 8 had the changed terms been in effect at the inception of the lease. Do the retroactive changes made effective from the inception date of the original lease cause the original lease to be classified on the basis of the changed terms?

The changes create a new lease agreement that must be classified on the basis of the revised terms on the date of the changes. If the new lease agreement is classified as an operating lease, a gain or loss will be recognized as provided by paragraph 14(a).

**Example 15**   When leases call for lower rental payments in the early years of the lease term that increase in later years, what modification is required when the early payments are not sufficient to cover the interest portion of the capitalized lease obligation?

The interest portion of the capitalized lease obligation should be charged on the interest method, which results in a constant rate of interest on the outstanding balance of the obligation over the amortization period (See paragraph 12).

This charge results in an accrual of unpaid interest in the early period of the lease when the lease payments are insufficient to cover the interest expense.

**Example 16**   Companies may arrange with Industrial Development Authorities (IDA) to have facilities financed by IDA bonds. The form of these transactions is such that, legally, the authority owns the property and the company is lessee. The lease typically calls for rental payments equal to the bond principal and interest, with an option to buy the property at any time for the amount required to retire the bonds outstanding. After the bonds are retired, title is transferred to the company for virtually no additional consideration. Before FASB No. 13, these arrangements were often capitalized as installment purchases and the underlying Authority bonds were recorded as though they were debts of the company. Does FASB No. 13 alter the accounting for these leases? Paragraph 16 of the Statement imposes disclosure requirements for all leases. Are these disclosures required when the property and bonds payable are reflected as described?

FASB No. 13 prescribes the appropriate accoutning and disclosure requirements for all lease transaction. When, however, the property and bond obligations have in the past been reflected directly on the balance sheet, auditors typically do not take exception provided the disclosures clearly indicate the facts relative to the lease.

**Example 17**    If a company presents consolidated financial statements accounts for the investment tax credit by the deferral method, can its leasing subsidiary adopt the flow-through method of accounting for the investment tax credit retained in connection with a sales-type lease?

Accounting Interpretation No. 6 of APB Opinion No. 4 (Investment Tax Credit in Consolidation) issued in March 1972 requires that a single method of accounting for the investment credit be adopted by a parent company and its subsidiaries in the consolidated financial statements (including subsidiaries carried on the equity method.)

The leasing subsidiary may adopt the flow-through method for the investment tax credit retained by it, but in consolidation the accounts of the subsidiary should be adjusted to reflect the single method reported on a consolidated basis.

**Example 18**    Must a manufacturer's wholly owned finance-leasing subsidiary engaged primarily in leasing property or equipment to unrelated parties be consolidated in the financial statements of the manufacturer?

FASB No. 13 (paragraph 31) requires consolidation of a leasing subsidiary only when the subsidiary's primary business activity is leasing property or facilities to the parent or an affiliated entity.

Questions are raised as to the propriety of excluding wholly owned finance-leasing subsidiaries from consolidated financial statements from the viewpoint that such practice omits substantial amounts of debt from the primary financial statements. Accounting Research Bulletin No. 51 (Consolidated Financial Statements) is the governing authority. Paragraph 3 thereof stipulates that separate statements would be preferable for subsidiaries if the presentation of financial information concerning the particular activities of such subsidiaries would be more informative than would inclusion of those subsidiaries in the consolidation. The Research Bulletin indicates that the equity method "may be preferable" for a finance company whose parent is a manufacturer.

In situations where a leasing subsidiary is accounted for by the equity method, condensed financial statements of the leasing subsidiary and the nature and terms of transactions between the parent and subsidiary should be disclosed in the consolidated financial statements of the parent.

The prevailing practice at this time permits the equity method of accounting for finance-leasing subsidiaries dealing with unrelated third parties. The FASB has placed this topic on its technical agenda and may eventually require consolidation.

**Example 19**    It is normal practice for manufacturers who have finance or leasing subsidiaries to sell manufactured equipment to the subsidiary at a price equivalent to that which an independent party would be charged. The subsidiary, in turn, enters into a financing type lease with an unaffiliated entity. How should the manufacturer account for this transaction?

In the consolidated financial statements, the manufacturer should recognize gross profit on the sale to the leasing subsidiary at the time the subsidiary consummates a lease that qualifies as a sales-type or direct financing lease with an unrelated party. Prior to that point, the sale of equipment to the subsidiary is intercompany and any profit thereon should be eliminated. The fact that the leasing subsidiary financed the purchase with nonrecourse debt would not alter this conclusion.

The substance of this transaction for the manufacturer is a sales-type lease between the manufacturer and the unrelated lessee. The gross profit to be recognized in the consolidated financial statements of the manufacturer should not exceed what would have been recognized under a sales-type lease between the manufacturer and the unrelated lessee.

Because of the way the transaction is structured, the limitation of the gross profit recognized in the consolidated financial statements of the manufacturer to what would have been recognized under a sales-type lease may involve cumbersome procedures. The transaction might be restructured so that the sales-type lease is recorded by the manufacturer at the point of sale and the investment in the lease could be transferred to the subsidiary.

**Example 20**    Does FASB No. 13 provide any guidance concerning the accounting for a lease of improved land?

Although it does not mention specifically land improvements, FASB No. 13 can be interpreted to deal with such improvements in the same manner that it deals with leases covering land and buildings. Land improvements are analogous to buildings in that they are depreciable property and are therefore consumed, at least in part, during the rental period. Paragraph 26 of FASB No. 13 should be followed in accounting for leases covering both depreciable and nondepreciable property.

# Chapter 3

# TAX ASPECTS OF LEASE FINANCING

As lease financing becomes an increasingly important part of a company's financial structure, the financial reporting and Federal income tax requirements related to leasing will require a larger share of management's time and effort. To complicate matters in the leasing area, differences exist between the financial accounting and tax accounting aspects of leasing. These differences may result from the treatment of a lease financing as a lease for tax purposes but as a sale or financing arrangement for accounting purposes. Prospective lessors and lessees should recognize the differing treatments and their effects.

FASB No. 13 classifies leases as either capital leases or operating leases. Capital leases are those that are substantially equivalent to purchases, while operating leases are more akin to the layman's understanding of the term "lease" (i.e., the use of an asset for some fixed, relatively short time period). FASB No. 13 outlines financial reporting requirements for each type of lease for both the lessee and the lessor. These requirements were discussed in Chapter 2.

## FEDERAL TAX REQUIREMENTS

Federal tax requirements differ from financial reporting requirements for leases. Federal tax requirements are based on Section 162(a)(3) of the Internal Revenue Code of 1954 (IRC), which provides that all the ordinary and necessary expenses paid or incurred during the taxable year in carrying on any trade or business are allowed as deductions. Such expenses include rentals or other payments required to be made as a condition to the continued use or possession, for purposes of the trade or business, of property to which the taxpayer has not taken or is not taking title or in which he has no equity.

The determination of whether an agreement represents a true lease or is in fact a conditional sales contract depends on the intent of the parties as evidenced by the provisions of the agreement, read in light of the facts and circumstances existing at the time the agreement was executed. No specific rule can be stated and no single test can be absolutely determinative. However, the Internal Revenue Service (IRS) has stated some guidelines for determining whether a transaction is a lease or a sale of property. The following discussion generally represents the position of the IRS; however, readers should carefully consider the specific circumstances of a lease when determining the tax treatment of the lease agreement.

### Factors Indicating a Sale

According to Revenue Ruling 55-540, in substance, a sale of property is indicated when one or more of the following has occurred:

1 Portions of periodic lease payments are made specifically applicable to an equity interest to be acquired by the lessee.
2 The lessee acquires title to the property.
3 The lease payments over a relatively short period constitute an inordinately large proportion of the amount needed to secure title.
4 The lease payments materially exceed the fair rental value.
5 A bargain purchase option is provided in the lease.
6 A part of the periodic payments is specifically designated or recognized as interest.
7 The lease payments plus the option price approximate the purchase price and provide for renewal of the lease at token amounts.
8 The lease payments over a short period of time approximate the purchase price and provide for renewal of the lease at token amounts.

The courts may treat a lease as a sale or a financing for tax purposes even though the lease agreement specifically excludes transfer of title. With respect to treatment of a lease as a conditional sales contract, Federal tax law takes priority over any state requirements regarding filing of security agreements.

Several matters should be given consideration in determining whether a true lease or a conditional sale has occurred. The fact that a lessee eventually purchases leased property does not necessarily mean that a conditional sale was intended at the inception of the lease. Rental deductions may be allowable on property that a lessee eventually purchases. A provision contained in the lease agreement stipulating that a portion of each rental payment will be applied to the purchase price of the property, if an option to buy is exercised, does not, by itself, create an ownership interest in the property for the lessee.

## Tax Effects of a Lease

When an intended lease is treated as a lease for federal income tax purposes, the lessor reports the rental income from the lease while the lessee receives a deduction for rent expense. The lessor also retains the right either to depreciate the asset and to receive the investment tax credit or to pass through the credit to the lessee.

## Tax Effects of a Sale

If a lease is treated as a conditional sale, the buyer (lessee) will be entitled to a depreciation deduction on the property, but not a rent deduction. The lessee's depreciation deduction will be computed over the useful life of the property and not simply over the lease term.

The lessee's basis in the property for depreciation purposes is the sum of all amounts that represent a part of the purchase price. Any part of the periodic payments that represents interest may be deductible by the lessee as interest expense. Section 483 of the Internal Revenue Code and the regulations under that section specify the manner in which interest expense is calculated.

When a lease is treated as a conditional sale, the lessee, as the owner of the property, is entitled to investment tax credits. In a case where the lease is treated as a conditional sale, the lessee is under no obligation to be sure that the lessor is handling its side of the transaction correctly for income tax purposes. In other words, the lessee can claim the investment credit even though the lessor may also be claiming the credit under an incorrect assumption that it is entitled to do so. If the lessee claims an investment credit, it must treat the transaction as a conditional sale from the inception of the lease. The lessee, as the owner for tax purposes, will also be entitled to deduct all other ordinary and necessary expenses that it pays or incurs.

If a conditional sale is deemed to have occurred, the lessor must show any gain realized on the sale. The lessor may be required to recognize the entire gain or may be able to use the installment method to report the gain. The lessor may also be required to report interest income under IRC Section 483.

The lessor will not be entitled to a deduction for depreciation if the lease is treated as a conditional sale. The lessor may instead have to recapture any depreciation it has previously taken under IRC Sections 1245 and 1250. The lessor may also have to recover any investment tax credits taken before the sale occurred. If the lessee is a governmental agency, the lessor may desire to have the lease transaction be treated as a conditional sale in order to take advantage of the tax-exempt interest provision of IRC Section 103.

## Comparative Analysis

Lease arrangements do not always represent rental contracts within the framework of financial reporting and federal tax requirements. Many lease agreements are, in substance, conditional sales contracts. In such conditional sale cases, the lessor will recognize a sale while the lessee will record a purchase. In addition, the lessee as the owner will record all the accounting entries pertaining to a sales agreement, that is, depreciation, interest expense, and any investment tax credit. Depreciation is computed over the estimated useful life of the property for federal tax purposes, although in some circumstances depreciation for financial reporting purposes is over the term of the lease.

Financial reporting and the tax requirements are similar in regard to the accounting treatment of lease agreements that have been classified as sales. Differences do exist in the determination of such classifications and in the treatment of interest expense. For financial reporting purposes, one of four criteria determine whether a lease will be classified as a sale or a financing. These four criteria relate to ownership, purchase options, economic life, and lease payments.

The tax requirements specify eight general criteria for classification of a lease as a sales agreement. Unlike the specific financial reporting criteria, these tax criteria are general in nature. Of the eight, five relate to lease payment characteristics, two concern ownership characteristics, and one pertains to a bargain purchase option. However, the intent of the parties is the most important indication of a true lease agreement.

In summary, leases may be classified as either rental agreements or sales/financing agreements. In those cases where leases are treated as sales agreements, a sale or purchase must be recorded and the transaction reflected as though ownership were transferred to the lessee. Each lease agreement should be evaluated in terms of the specifics of the agreement, the intent of the parties and the criteria set forth by FASB No. 13 and IRS requirements.

## Tax Effects of a Sale and Leaseback

Certain financial and professional reasons may induce a taxpayer to pay rent on business property rather than to seek ownership of the property outright, for example, a need for working capital that would otherwise be tied up in the ownership of property. In such cases, the taxpayer may decide to sell the property or perhaps place the property in trust for his or her children and then lease it back. Such transactions are referred to as sale and leaseback or gift and leaseback transactions. Since these transactions also bring with them some tax advantages, such as additional business deductions or income splitting with members of a family, they attract the scrutiny of the IRS, particularly if the property is sold or given to a related taxpayer (spouse, stockholder, etc.). If the transfer is made solely to avoid taxes, the transfer will not be recognized. Numerous court decisions have revolved about the question of whether such transactions are tax avoidance schemes.

In determining whether particular transactions are based on a tax avoidance, the courts have looked to the particular circumstances of each case. There have been three criteria employed in making this determination. The first two are common to both sale and gift cases, while the third is specific to the gift/trust situation.

*Lack of Equity Interest*    Code Section 162(a) (3) specifically provides that, in order for a rental deduction to be proper, the taxpayer cannot hold title or have an equitable interest in the property in question. Thus, for example, the keeping of a reversionary interest has been construed to represent an equity interest and has led to the disallowance of a deduction for rent paid to a trust.

*Business Purpose*    A business purpose must be present, with the sale being grounded in economic reality. Some courts have distinguished between a business purpose and economic reality as two separate concepts. However, the two concepts are closely related. In situations involving trusts, a court may consider the business purpose condition to be fulfilled if the business reason for the transaction is apparent after the gift to the trust has been made. Other courts, however, will view the gift and leaseback as an integrated transaction and insist that the business purpose be present at the time the gift was made. It should be noted that this is an area where the reasonableness of the rent paid will be considered in determining whether there was a legitimate business transaction.

*Independent Trustee*    In assessing the good faith of a gift to a trust and the subsequent leaseback, a crucial factor is the independence of the trustee. Where control has remained in the hands of the donor, the deductions may be disallowed.

The deductibility of the rental payments in trust and leaseback transactions, where the donor keeps a reversionary interest or a certain degree of control, remains a prime issue for the IRS, meaning that the IRS will ordinarily litigate this question.

The question of whether a sale and leaseback is a valid sale and a true lease for tax purposes has been discussed in recent years by the Supreme Court. A landmark case in this area is the Lyons case *(Frank Lyon Co. v. U.S., 98* Supreme Court 1291). In this case the Supreme Court decided that "where there is a genuine multiple-party transaction with economic substance which is compelled or encouraged by business or regulatory realities, is imbued with tax-independent considerations, and is not shaped solely by tax avoidance features that have meaningless labels attached, Government should honor allocation of rights and duties effectuated by the parties."

## Sale Distinguished from Lease with Option to Purchase

Where a lease contains an option to purchase, the question arises as to whether the transaction should be treated as an installment sale contract for tax purposes rather than a lease. As discussed previously, if the lease is regarded as a conditional sale contract, the rental payments will not be deductible by the user of the equipment, either in full or to the extent that the payment is in excess of a reasonable rental. The user will be required to capitalize the lease payments, or at least the disallowed portion, and will be entitled to deduct depreciation. From the standpoint of the seller-lessor, the question of whether there has been a true lease or a conditional sale will determine whether the payments are ordinary income or capital gain if the equipment is a capital asset. Where the equipment involved is stock in trade or other inventory property of the seller-lessor or property held by the seller-lessor for sale to customers in the ordinary course of a trade or business, the gain would be ordinary income to the seller-lessor whether the transaction is a true lease or a conditional sale.

A lease with an option to purchase offers the advantage of immediate rental deductions, which can be larger than depreciation allowances on the same equipment. In a lease with a purchase option, the taxpayer's right to take title to the equipment is retained, a business advantage that an ordinary lease without a purchase option would not offer. The problem is to keep the option price high enough, or the rental payments low enough, so that for tax purposes the rent will not be treated as a partial payment toward the purchase price.

In lease with option cases, the Tax Court has often applied an "economic reality" or "intent to purchase" test. If the option is exercisable within a period that is less than the useful life of the property and the rental payments cover a substantial part of what would be the purchase price, the Tax Court may hold that a sale and purchase are intended.

How to treat excessive rent where there is no actual sale can be a problem. It should be noted that if the only objection to a Code Section 162 deduction is the amount involved, the customary procedure is to determine what amount is a "reasonable" deduction and allow that much at least. Therefore, some amount would be deductible even though the rentals paid would be considered to be excessive.

How the excess, or disallowed, portion of the rent paid in such a situation would be handled for income tax purposes is a more difficult problem and one for which there are no established precedents. The question is whether it can be capitalized on some theory or whether the entire benefit of that portion of the rent is lost for income tax purposes.

Perhaps the most effective contention a taxpayer could make (as an alternative to simply conceding that deduction of part of the rent is improper) would be that the "excess" rent is, in effect, the consideration paid in order to obtain and keep alive the option of purchasing the property. This would not add to his current deductions, but it would identify the payment as part of the ultimate cost basis resulting from exercise of the option, and it would not be inconsistent with the contention that the reasonable portion of the rent is actually rent, rather than a part of the purchase price of the property.

This position might be made stronger, if the reasonableness of the rent seems questionable, by making provision in the lease for two separate types of payments: (1) a specified amount of rent, plus (2) an additional amount (equal to the difference between the total payment agreed on and the lesser amount that would normally be considered "reasonable") required as consideration for the option, the lease making it clear that this additional payment confers no equity in the property. In addition, under Section 483 of the code, it may be possible to characterize the excess portion as interest, which would be deductible as interest expense.

The Internal Revenue Service, in 1955, issued three rulings regarding the tax status of payments under leases of equipment. One ruling (Revenue Ruling 55-540) contains a comprehensive analysis of provisions in typical leases and references to decided cases. The other two refer to specific lease cases. The reader should refer to these revenue rulings for further guidance in the equipment leasing area. See Revenue Ruling 55-540, C.B. 1955-2; Revenue Ruling 55-541, C.B. 1955-2; Revenue Ruling 55-542, C.B. 1955-2.

## Leveraged Leases

A leveraged lease is a transaction in which a lessor borrows money to purchase property and then leases that property to a lessee. The IRS has issued guidelines to determine whether leases involving leverage will be considered as true leases for Federal income tax purposes.

In general, for a leveraged lease to be treated as a true lease for tax purposes:

1 The lessor must have made a minimum "at risk" investment in the property that is unconditional and that will last from the beginning through the end of the lease term.

2 No member of the lessee group may have a contractual right to purchase the property at less than the fair market value at the time of the exercise of that right nor may the lessor have a contractual right to force a purchase.

3 No member of the lessee group may either invest in the property or lend money to the lessor towards its purchase.

4 The lessor must expect a profit from the transaction apart from any tax advantages.

A taxpayer may seek an advanced ruling with respect to the tax treatment of a leveraged lease. The procedures for doing so are discussed in IRS guidelines contained in Revenue Procedure 75-28, 1975-1 C.B. 752.

It is prudent to seek an advance ruling from the IRS in a leveraged lease situation in those cases where:

1   The transaction is essentially a means of financing the acquisition of equipment on the part of the lessee.

2   The lessors are tax oriented investors.

3   The equipment is expensive or composed of large fleets (e.g., aircraft, railroad cars).

4   A bank is involved as the lessor or as the lender to the lessor.

In many cases, a bank lessor will require that an advanced ruling be obtained for any lease transaction above a certain size, for example, $5 million. Although management may participate in the preparation of necessary data and documents to seek an advance ruling, success in expediting the process is often obtained through the employment of attorneys who specialize in this particular area of the tax law.

### REVENUE RULING 55–540

#### Section 1   Purpose

The purpose of this ruling is to state the position of the Internal Revenue Service regarding the income tax aspects of the purported leasing of equipment for use in the trade or business of the lessee.

#### Section 2   Background

.01   Apart from other business reasons for entering into leases of equipment instead of outright purchases, a significant motive may, in some cases, be the tax advantages which might result because of the different timing of the deductions for rent as compared to depreciation. In this ruling the terms "lessor" and "lessee" are used for convenience, without intending to suggest the proper characterization of any agreement.

.02   The agreements are generally cast in the form of chattel leases. They may be grouped as follows:

    **(a)**   Short-term agreements which usually concern mobile equipment or relatively small articles of equipment. The "compensation for use" provisions in these agreements are usually expressed in terms of an hourly, daily, or weekly rental, and the rental rates are relatively high in relation to the value of the article. There may be an option to purchase the equipment at a price fixed in advance which will approximate the fair market value of the equipment at the time of the election to exercise the option. In this type of agreement, all costs of repairs, maintenance, taxes, insurance, etc., are obligations of the lessor.

**(b)** Agreements entered into by taxpayers engaged in the business of leasing personal property to others either as their principal business activity or incidental thereto. Under the terms of these agreements the amounts payable, called rental rates, are ordinarily based on normal operations or use, plus a surcharge for operations in excess of the normal stated usage. In some instances, the rental is based on units produced or mileage operated. Termination of the agreement at stated periods is provided upon due notice by either party. If the agreement includes an option to purchase, the option price has no relation to the amounts paid as rentals.

**(c)** Agreements providing for a "rental" over a comparatively short period of time in relation to the life of the equipment. The agreed "rental" payments fully cover the normal purchase price plus interest. Title usually passes to the lessee upon the payment of a stated amount of "rental" or on termination of the agreement upon the payment of an amount which when added to the "rental" paid approximates the normal purchase price of the equipment plus interest.

**(d)** Agreements which provide for the payment of "rental" for a short original term in relation to the expected life of the equipment, with provision for continued use over substantially all of the remaining useful life of the equipment. During the initial term of the agreement, the "rental" approximates the normal purchase price of the equipment, plus interest, while the "rentals" during the remaining term or renewal period or periods are insignificant when compared to the initial rental. These agreements may or may not provide for an option to acquire legal title to the equipment upon the termination of the initial period or at any stated time thereafter.

**(e)** Agreements similar to the arrangement in (d) above, but with the added factor that the manufacturer of the equipment purports to sell it to a credit or finance company, which either takes an assignment of such an existing agreement with the user or itself later enters into such an agreement with the user. In some instances, the lessor may be a trustee acting for the original vendor.

## Section 3   Nature of the Problem

**.01**   Deductible trade or business expenses include rental expenses for use of property to which the taxpayer has not taken or is not taking title or in which he has no equity.

**.02** In deciding whether a taxpayer is entitled to deduction for rentals it is necessary to determine whether by virtue of the agreement the lessee has acquired, or will acquire, title to or an equity in the property. The determination of that question with respect to agreements of the type here involved will ordinarily depend upon whether the particular agreement should be treated as in reality a lease or a conditional sale contract.

## Section 4   Determination Whether an Agreement Is a Lease or a Conditional Sales Contract

**.01**   Whatever interest is obtained by a lessee is acquired under the terms of the agreement itself. Whether an agreement, which in form is a lease, is in substance a conditional sales contract depends upon the intent of the parties as evidenced by the provisions of the agreement, read in the light of the facts and circumstances existing at the time the agreement was executed. In ascertaining such intent no single test, or any special combination of tests is absolutely determinative. No general rule, applicable to all cases, can be laid down. Each case must be decided in the light of its particular facts. However, in the absence of compelling persuasive factors of contrary implication, an intent warranting treatment of a transaction for tax purposes as a purchase and sale rather than as a lease or rental agreement may in general be said to exist if, for example, one or more of the following conditions are present:

**(a)**   Portions of the periodic payments are made specifically applicable to an equity to be acquired by the lessee. (*Truman Bowen*, 12 TC 446, Dec. Dec. 16,877 (Acq.).)

**(b)**   The lessee will acquire title upon the payment of a stated amount of "rentals" which under the contract he is required to make. (*Robert A. Taft*, 27 BTA 808, Dec. 7944; *Truman Bowen, supra.*)

**(c)**   The total amount which the lessee is required to pay for a relatively short period of use constitutes an inordinately large proportion of the total sum required to be paid to secure the transfer of the title. (*Truman Bowen, supra.*)

**(d)**   The agreed "rental" payments materially exceed the current fair rental value. This may be indicative that the payments include an element other than compensation for the use of property. (*McWaters, Truman Bowen, supra.*)

**(e)**   The property may be acquired under a purchase option at a price which is nominal in relation to the value of the property at the time when the option may be exercised, as determined at the time of entering into the original agreement, or which is a relatively small amount when compared with the total payments which are required to be made. (*Holeproof Hosiery Co.* Compare *H.T. Benton*, (CA-5) 52-1 VSTC ¶9367, 197 F. 2d 745.)

**(f)**   Some portion of the periodic payments is specifically designated as interest or is otherwise readily recognizable as the equivalent of interest. (*Judson Mills.*)

**.02** The fact that the agreement makes no provision for the transfer of title or specifically precludes the transfer of title does not, of itself, prevent the contract from being held to be a sale of an equitable interest in the property.

**.03** Conditional sales of personal property are, in general, recordable under the various State Recording Acts if the vendor wishes to protect its lien against claims of creditors. However, the recording or failure to record such a sales contract is usually discretionary with the vendor and is not controlling insofar as the essential nature of the contract is concerned for Federal tax purposes.

**.04** Agreements are usually indicative of an intent to rent the equipment if the rental payments are at an hourly, daily, or weekly rate or are based on production, use, mileage, or a similar measure and are not directly related to the normal purchase price, provided, if there is an option to purchase, that the price at which the equipment may be acquired reasonably approximates the anticipated fair market value on the option date. Thus, agreements of the type, described in section 2.02(a) and (b), above, will usually be considered leases, in the absence of other facts or circumstances which denote a passing of title or an equity interest to the lessee.

**.05** In the absence of compelling factors indicating a different intent, it will be presumed that a conditional sales contract was intended if the total of the rental payments and any option price payable in addition thereto approximates the price at which the equipment could have been acquired by purchase at the time of entering into the agreement, plus interest and/or carrying charges. Agreements of the type described in section 2.02(c), above, will generally be held to be sales of the equipment.

**.06** If the sum of the specified "rentals" over a relatively short part of the expected useful life of the equipment approximates the price at which the equipment could have been acquired by purchase at the time of entering into the agreement, plus interest and/or carrying charges on such amount, and the lessee may continue to use the equipment for an additional period or periods approximating its remaining estimated useful life for relatively nominal or token payments, it may be assumed that the parties have entered into a sale contract, even though a passage of title is not expressly provided in the agreement. Agreements of the type described in section 2.02(d) and (e), above, in general, will be held to be sales contracts.

**Section 5     Reporting of Income and Deductions by a Lessor or a Vendor**

**.01** The amounts paid for the use of equipment under an agreement which is determined under the foregoing principles, to be a lease will be held to be rental income to the lessor. Such lessor may deduct all ordinary and necessary expenses paid or incurred during the taxable year which are attributable to the earning of the income. In addition, the lessor will be allowed a deduction for depreciation. If the lessee under the contract pays to the lessor a stipulated rental, and in addition pays certain other expenses which are properly payable by the lessor, the lessor is deemed to have received as rental income not only the stipulated rental but also the amount of such other expenses paid by the lessee to, or for the amount of, the lessor, except as provided in Code Sec. 110.

**.02** If the agreement is determined to be a sale, the amounts received under the contract by the vendor will be considered to be payments on the sales price of the equipment to the extent such amounts do not represent interest or other charges.

### Section 6    Deductions Allowable to Lessee or Purchaser

**.01** If it is held, under the foregoing principles, that an agreement is a lease, the lessee may deduct the amount of rent paid or accrued, including all expenses which under the terms of the agreement the lessee is required to pay to, for, or on account of the lessor, except as provided by Code Sec. 110. If the payments are so arranged as to constitute advance rental, such payments will be duly apportioned over the lease term. In computing the term of the lease, all options to renew shall be taken into consideration if there is a reasonable expectation that such options will be exercised.

**.02** If under the provisions of this Revenue Ruling the agreement is to be treated as a sale, the amounts paid to the vendor will be considered as payments for the purchase of the equipment to the extent such amounts do not represent interest or other charges. Expenditures treated as payments for the purchase of the equipment may be recovered over the life of the asset through appropriate depreciation deductions.

### Section 7    Illustration

The taxpayer leased a used tractor with dozer. It was to pay for all necessary repairs, taxes and insurance, and was given an option to purchase the equipment by paying the balance of the monthly rentals due under the contract plus $1.00. The taxpayer exercised the option. The payments were not rental payments, but were partial payments of the purchase price. *Quartzite Stone Co.*, 30 TC 511, Dec. 23,012, aff'd on other grounds, (CA-10) 60-1 USTC 9211, 273 F. 2d 738.

### LEVERAGED LEASES—REVENUE RULING 75-21

### Section 1    Purpose

The purpose of this Revenue Procedure is to set forth guidelines that the Internal Revenue Service will use for advance ruling purposes in determining whether certain transactions purporting to be leases of property are, in fact, leases for Federal income tax purposes. The type of transaction covered by this Revenue Procedure is commonly called a "leveraged lease." Such a lease transaction generally involves three parties: a lessor, a lessee and a lender to the lessor. In general, these leases are not leases, the lease term covers a substantial part of the useful life of the leased property, and the lessee's payments to the lessor are sufficient to discharge the lessor's payments to the lender.

## Section 2   Background

Section 4.01 of Rev. Rul. 55-540, 1955-2 C. B. 39 sets forth certain conditions that, in the absence of compelling factors of contrary implication, would warrant treatment of a transaction for Federal income tax purposes as a conditional sales contract rather than a lease of equipment. See Rev. Rul. 55-541, 1955-2 C. B. 19; Rev. Rul. 55-542, 1955-2 C. B. 59; and Rev. Rul. 57-371, 1957-2 C.B. 214, for examples of transactions determined to be sales rather than leases. See Rev. Rul. 60-122, 1960-1 C.B. 56 for two transactions, one considered a lease and the other considered a sale. See also Rev. Rul. 72-408, 1972-2 C.B. 86, concerning the Federal income tax consequences of a transaction cast in the form of a lease subsequently determined to be a sale.

## Section 3   Nature of the Problem

Rev. Rul. 55-540, cited above, provides guidelines for determining the existence of a conditional sales contract but does not contain guidelines for determining the existence of a lease. The guidelines set forth in Section 4 of this Revenue Procedure are being published to clarify the circumstances in which an advance ruling recognizing the existence of a lease ordinarily will be issued and thus to provide assistance to taxpayers in preparing ruling requests and to assist the Service in issuing advance ruling letters as promptly as practicable. These guidelines do not define, as a matter of law, whether a transaction is or is not a lease for Federal income tax purposes and are not intended to be used for audit purposes. If these guidelines are not satisfied, the Service nevertheless will consider ruling in appropriate cases on the basis of all the facts and circumstances.

## Section 4   Guidelines

Unless other facts and circumstances indicate a contrary intent, for advance ruling purposes only, the Service will consider the lessor in a leveraged lease transaction to be the owner of the property and the transaction a valid lease if all the following conditions are met.

*(1)   Minimum Unconditional "At Risk" Investment*   The lessor must have made a minimum unconditional "at risk" investment in the property (the "Minimum Investment") when the lease begins, must maintain such Minimum Investment throughout the entire lease term, and such Minimum Investment must remain at the end of the lease term. The Minimum Investment must be an equity investment (the "Equity Investment") which, for purposes of this Revenue Procedure, includes only consideration paid and personal liability incurred by the lessor to purchase the property. The net worth of the lessor must be sufficient to satisfy any such

personal liability. In determining the lessor's Minimum Investment, the following rules will be applied:

(A) *Initial Minimum Investment*   When the property is first placed in service or use by the lessee, the Minimum Investment must be equal to at least 20 percent of the cost of the property. The Minimum Investment must be unconditional. That is, after the property is first placed in service or use by the lessee, the lessor must not be entitled to a return of any portion of the Minimum Investment through any arrangement, directly or indirectly, with the lessee, a shareholder of the lessee, or any party related to the lessee (within the meaning of section 318 of the Internal Revenue Code of 1954) (the "Lessee Group"). The lease transaction may include an arrangement with someone other than the foregoing parties that provides for such a return to the lessor if the property fails to satisfy written specifications for the supply, construction, or manufacture of the property.

(B) *Maintenance of Minimum Investment*   The Minimum Investment must remain equal to at least 20 percent of the cost of the property at all times throughout the entire lease term. That is, the excess of the cumulative payments required to have been paid by the lessee to or on behalf of the lessor over the cumulative disbursements required to have been paid by or for the lessor in connection with the ownership of the property must never exceed the sum of (i) any excess of the lessor's initial Equity Investment over 20 percent of the cost of the property plus (ii) the cumulative pro rata portion of the projected profit from the transaction (exclusive of tax benefits).

(C) *Residual Investment*   The lessor must represent and demonstrate that an amount equal to at least 20 percent of the original cost of the property is a reasonable estimate of what the fair market value of the property will be at the end of the lease term. For this purpose, fair market value must be determined (i) without including in such value any increase or decrease for inflation or deflation during the lease term, and (ii) after subtracting from such value any cost to the lessor for removal and delivery of possession of the property to the lessor at the end of the lease term. In addition, the lessor must represent and demonstrate that a remaining useful life of the longer of one year or 20 percent of the originally estimated useful life of the property is a reasonable estimate of what the remaining useful life of the property will be at the end of the lease term.

*(2)  Lease Term and Renewal Options*   For purposes of this Revenue Procedure, the lease term includes all renewal or extension periods except renewals or extensions at the option of the lessee at fair rental value at the time of such renewal or extension.

*(3) Purchase and Sale Rights* No member of the Lessee Group may have a contractual right to purchase the property from the lessor at a price less than its fair market value at the time the right is exercised. When the property is first placed in service or use by the lessee, the lessor may not have a contractual right (except as provided in section 4(1)(A) above) to cause any party to purchase the property. The lessor must also represent that it does not have any present intention to acquire such a contractual right. The effect of any such right acquired at a subsequent time will be determined at that time based on all the facts and circumstances. A provision that permits the lessor to abandon the property to any party will be treated as a contractual right of the lessor to cause such party to purchase the property.

*(4) No Investment by Lessee* No part of the cost of the property may be furnished by any member of the Lessee Group. Nor may any such party furnish any part of the cost of improvement or additions to the property, except for improvements or additions that are owned by any member of the Lessee Group and are readily removable without causing material damage to the property. Any item that is so readily removable must not be subject to a contract or option for purchase or sale between the lessor and any member of the Lessee Group at a price other than its fair market value at the time of such purchase or sale. However:

(A) *Cost Overruns and Modifications* If the cost of property exceeds the estimate on which the lease was based, the lease may provide for adjustment of the rents to compensate the lessor for such additional cost (but see section 5.01 concerning uneven rent payments).

(B) *Maintenance and Repair* If the lease requires the lessee to maintain and keep the property in good repair during the term of the lease, ordinary maintenance and repairs performed by the lessee will not constitute an improvement or addition to the property.

*(5) No Lessee Loans or Guarantees* No member of the Lessee Group may lend to the lessor any of the funds necessary to acquire the property, or guarantee any indebtedness created in connection with the acquisition of the property by the lessor. A guarantee by any member of the Lessee Group of the lessee's obligation to pay rent, properly maintain the property, or pay insurance premiums or other similar conventional obligations of a net lease does not constitute the guarantee of the indebtedness of the lessor.

*(6) Profit Requirement* The lessor must represent and demonstrate that it expects to receive a profit from the transaction, apart from the value of or benefits obtained from the tax deductions, allowances, credits and other tax attributes arising from such transaction. This requirement is met if:

The aggregate amount required to be paid by the lessee to or for the lessor over the lease term plus the value of the residual investment referred to in

Section 4(1)(C) above exceed an amount equal to the sum of the aggregate disbursements required to be paid by or for the lessor in connection with the ownership of the property and the lessor's Equity Investment in the property, including any direct costs to finance the Equity Investment and the aggregate amounts required to be paid to or for the lessor over the lease term exceed by a reasonable amount the aggregate disbursements required to be paid by or for the lessor in connection with the ownership of the property.

## Section 5    Other Considerations

**.01**    Leveraged lease transactions that satisfy the guidelines set forth in Section 4 hereof nevertheless may contain uneven rent payments that result in prepaid or deferred rent. The Service ordinarily will not raise any question about prepaid or deferred rent if the annual rent for any year (i) is not more than 10 percent above or below the amount calculated by dividing the total rent payable over the lease term by the number of years in such term, or (ii) during at least the first two-thirds of the lease term is not more than 10 percent above or below the amount calculated by dividing the total rent payable over such initial portion of the lease term by the number of years in such initial portion of the lease term, and if the annual rent for any year during the remainder of the lease term is no greater than the highest annual rent for any year during the initial portion of the lease term and no less than one-half of the average annual rent during such initial portion of the lease term. Any ruling request involving uneven rent payments that do not satisfy the above exceptions must contain a request for a ruling as to whether any portion of the uneven rent payments is prepaid or deferred rent. Any ruling issued by the Service as to the existence of a lease may contain an appropriate ruling or caveat as to such prepaid or deferred rent.

**.02**    The Service has not decided whether rulings will be issued with respect to property that is expected not to be useful or usable by the lessor at the end of the lease term except for purposes of continued leasing or transfer to any member of the Lessee Group. Prior to the final decision, consideration will be given to any comments pertaining thereto that are submitted in writing (preferably six copies) to the Commissioner of Internal Revenue at the address in Section 7 below by May 30, 1975. Designations of material as confidential or not to be disclosed contained in such comments will not be accepted. Thus a person submitting written comments should not include therein material that is considered to be confidential or inappropriate for disclosure to the public. It will be presumed by the Internal Revenue Service that every written comment submitted to it in response to this request is intended by the person submitting it to be subject in its entirety to public inspection and copying in accordance with the same procedures as are prescribed in 26 CFR 601.702(d)(9) for public inspection and copying of written comments received in response to a notice of proposed rule making.

### Section 6    Effective Date

The provisions of this Revenue Procedure are effective with respect to those requests received after May 5, 1975.

### Section 7    Inquiries

Inquiries regarding this Revenue Procedure should refer to its number and be addressed to the Commissioner of Internal Revenue, 1111 Constitution Avenue, N.W., Washington, D.C. 20224, Attention: T:C:C. Rev. Proc. 75-21, announced in T. I. R. No. 1362, April 11, 1975, 759 CCH 6529.

## LEVERAGED LEASES—REVENUE PROCEDURE 75-28

### Section 1    Purpose

This Revenue Procedure concerns requests for advanced rulings on leveraged lease transactions within the meaning of Rev. Proc. 75-21, 1975-18 I. R. B. 15. Rev. Proc. 75-21 sets forth guidelines to be used for advance ruling purposes in determining whether such a transaction is, in fact, a lease for Federal income tax purposes. The purpose of this Revenue Procedure is to set forth the information and representations required to be furnished by the taxpayers in a request for such a ruling. The specific terms used in this Revenue Procedure are defined in Rev. Proc. 75-21.

### Section 2    Background

.01    The Internal Revenue Service receives many requests for rulings on leveraged leases. Frequently the information that is necessary for consideration of the issues presented is not included in the initial ruling requests, and since substantive processing of such cases cannot begin until the required information is obtained, this results in unnecessary delays in the issuance of rulings. The checklist set forth in this Revenue Procedure is designed to ensure the inclusion and order of presentation of necessary information in the initial ruling request. However, since the information necessary for the issuance of a ruling with regard to any particular transaction depends upon all the facts and circumstances of that case, information in addition to that outlined in the checklist may be required with respect to that transaction.

.02    In view of the complexity of a typical leveraged lease transaction and the voluminous nature of the related documentation, the Service cannot accept the responsibility for raising or considering issues arising out of such provisions that are not specifically brought to its attention. See sections 6 and 13 of Rev. Proc. 72-3, 1972-1 C.B. 698.

### Section 3   General Requirements

**.01**   The lessor and the lessee and any other party with an interest in the leasing transaction for whom a specific ruling is requested must join in the ruling request.

**.02**   The ruling request must include a summary statement of the facts as described in section 6.03 of Rev. Proc. 72-3, 1972-1 C.B. 698, relating to the "two-part" ruling request procedure.

**.03**   In addition to the information and documents required by section 6 of Rev. Proc. 72-3, the ruling request must include detailed information required by section 4 of this Revenue Procedure. If the information requested is not applicable to the parties or to the transaction, an express statement to that effect is required. The response to each item of information requested must include a reference to the page number of any relevant document containing the information that supports the response. Furthermore, portions of the relevant documents supporting a particular response should be underscored or otherwise highlighted and cross-referenced to the appropriate subsection of section 4 of this Revenue Procedure. All parties joining in the request for ruling are jointly responsible for responses to each item of information requested by section 4 of this Revenue Procedure, with the exception of section 4.02 for which only the lessor is responsible.

**.04**   The lessor must also submit copies of any offering circular, prospectus, economic analysis, or other document used to induce the lessor's investment in the leased property (the "Property"). These documents must include an analysis of the projected cash flow to the lessor from the lease transaction including the projected benefits from the tax attributes thereof.

### Section 4   Specific Information Required

#### *.01   In General*

1   Describe in detail the type and quantity of the leased Property.

2   Describe all parties to the leveraged lease transaction, their respective interests in such transaction, and the relationships that exist between or among such parties.

3   Submit a diagram of the transaction showing (1) the parties to the transaction, (2) the succession of ownership to the Property, and (3) the source, amounts, and flow of the funds used to acquire the Property (total acquisition cost within the meaning of section 1012 of the Internal Revenue Code of 1954).

4   Indicate whether the Property is to be temporarily or permanently affixed to or installed on or in land, buildings, or other property. If so, indicate who will own such land, buildings, or other property.

5   Indicate whether the Property is new, reconstructed, used, or rebuilt. (*See* sections 1.48-2 and 1.48-3 of the regulations; Rev. Rul. 68-111, 1968-1 C.B. 29; and Rev. Rul. 70-135, 1970-1 C.B. 10.)

**6** Indicate when, where, and how the Property will be, or has been, first placed in service or use.

*.02 Minimum Unconditional "At Risk" Investment* The lessor must:

**1** Indicate the total acquisition cost (within the meaning of section 1012 of the Code) of the Property.

**2** Indicate when and in what amounts the lessor did or will make its Equity Investment or incur personal liability for such Equity Investment.

**3** Indicate the conditions under which the lessor would be entitled to a return of any portion of its Equity Investment or would be released from any personal liability for such Equity Investment.

**4** Submit a representation of the net worth of the lessor and financial data to support the representation, including, for example, audited balance sheets or unaudited balance sheets with a representation that the latter are prepared in accordance with generally accepted accounting principles.

**5** Submit an analysis demonstrating that the lessor's Equity Investment will remain equal to at least 20 percent of the cost of the Property at all times throughout the lease term. This analysis must demonstrate that throughout the lease term the items designated as (a), (b), (c) and (d) solve the formula:

$$(a) - (b) \text{ never exceeds } (c) + (d)$$

    **(a)** The projected cumulative payments required to be paid by the lessee to or for the lessor.

    **(b)** The projected cumulative disbursements required to be paid by or for the lessor in connection with the ownership of the Property, excluding the lessor's initial Equity Investment, but including any direct costs to finance the Equity Investment.

    **(c)** The excess of lessor's initial Equity Investment over 20 percent of the cost of the Property.

    **(d)** A cumulative pro rata portion of the projected profits from the transaction (exclusive of tax benefits). Profit for this purpose is the excess of the sum of (i) the amounts required to be paid by the lessee to or for the lessor over the lease term plus (ii) the value of the residual investment referred to in section 4(1)(C) of Rev. Proc. 75-21, over the aggregate disbursements required to be paid by or for the lessor in connection with the ownership of the Property, including the lessor's initial Equity Investment and any direct costs to finance the Equity Investment.

**6** Furnish an opinion, from a qualified expert who has professional knowledge of the type of property subject to the lease, regarding:

    **(a)** the fair market value of the Property at the end of the lease term, determined in accordance with section 4(1)(C) of Rev. Proc. 75-21, and the manner in which such fair market value was determined;

    **(b)** the cost to the lessor, if any, of the removal and delivery of possession of the Property to the lessor at the end of the lease term; and

(c)   the remaining useful life of the Property at the end of the lease term, and the manner in which such useful life was determined.

*.03   Lease Term and Renewal Options*   Indicate the period for which the Property will be leased initially, whether there are any provisions for the renewal or extension of such period and, if so, on what terms.

*.04   Purchase and Sale Rights*

1   Indicate whether any member of the Lessee Group or any other party has a contractual obligation or right to purchase all or any part of the Property at any time, and, if so, when, under what conditions, and at what price.

2   Indicate whether the lessor or any other party has a contractual right to cause any party to purchase the Property, and if so, when and under what conditions.

3   Indicate whether the lessor, a shareholder of the lessor, or a party related to the lessor (within the meaning of section 318 of the Code), or any other party who has joined in the request for a ruling has any present intention to acquire a contractual right to cause any party to purchase or sell the Property and, if so, when and under what conditions.

4   Indicate whether the lessor may abandon the Property to any party at any time, and if so, when, to whom, and under what conditions.

*.05   No Investment by Lessee*

1   Indicate whether any member of the Lessee Group may be required to furnish any part of the cost of the Property or the cost of improvements, modifications, or additions to the Property, and if so, when and under what conditions.

2   If improvements, modifications, or additions are made or are to be made to the Property, indicate who will own such improvements, modifications, or additions.

3   Indicate whether such improvements, modifications, or additions may be removed from the Property without causing material damage to the Property.

4   Indicate whether the transaction contains any cost overrun provisions and who must pay the cost overrun.

5   Indicate whether the lease provides for an adjustment to rents to compensate the lessor for any additional cost incurred because of cost overruns, improvements, modifications, or additions to the Property.

6   Identify all other parties who provided or will provide funds necessary to purchase any improvements, modifications, or additions to the Property, and the amounts of any resulting indebtedness.

*.06   No Lessee Loans or Guarantees*

1   Indicate whether any member of the Lessee Group will guarantee any indebtedness incurred in connection with the acquisition of the Property by the lessor and, if so, under what terms and conditions.

**2** Indicate whether any member of the Lessee Group directly or indirectly made or will make any other guarantees as a part or result of the lease transaction. If so, describe such guarantees.

### .07 *Profit Requirement*

**1** Submit an analysis demonstrating that the lessor will receive a profit from the transaction exclusive of benefits from the tax attributes thereof. This analysis should demonstrate that the terms identified as (a), (b), and (c) will solve the formula:

$$(a) + (b) \text{ exceed } (c).$$

**(a)** The projected aggregate payments required to be paid by the lessee to or for the lessor over the lease term.

**(b)** The value of the residual investment described in section 4(1)(C) of Rev. Proc. 75-21.

**(c)** The projected sum of the aggregate disbursements required to be paid by or for the lessor in connection with the ownership of the Property, including the lessor's initial Equity Investment and any direct costs to finance the Equity Investment.

**2** Submit an analysis demonstrating that the lessor will have a projected positive cash flow from the lease transaction. This analysis must contain the following information in order to demonstrate that the items identified as (a) and (b) will solve the formula:

$$(a) \text{ exceeds } (b) \text{ by a reasonable minimum amount.}$$

**(a)** The projected aggregate payments required to be paid by the lessee to or for the lessor over the lease term.

**(b)** The projected aggregate disbursements required to be paid by or for the lessor in connection with the ownership of the Property, excluding the lessor's initial Equity Investment, but including any direct costs to finance the Equity Investment.

### .08 *Other Considerations: Uneven Rent*

**1** Submit an analysis demonstrating that the annual rent to be paid always will be within a range of 10 percent above or below the average annual rent computed by dividing the total annual rent payable over the lease term by the numbers of years in such term.

**2** If the test indicated in section 4.081 cannot be met, prepare an analysis that demonstrates whether the annual rents come within the limits set forth in (a) and (b) below.

**(a)** During the initial portion of the lease term (a period of at least two-thirds of the lease term), the annual rent always will be within a range of 10 percent above or below the amount determined to be the average annual rent for such initial portion of the lease term. The average annual rent for such initial portion is calculated by dividing the total annual rent payable over such initial portion by the number of years in such initial portion.

(b) The annual rent for any year of the lease term following such initial portion is no greater than the highest annual rent for any year during such initial portion and no less than one-half of the average annual rent during such initial portion.

3   If neither test in section 4.081 or 4.082 above can be met, then a ruling whether any portion of the uneven rent payments is prepaid or deferred rent must be requested and a complete explanation submitted as to why the rent payments are uneven.

### .09   Other Considerations: Limited Use Property

1   Indicate whether the Property is expected to be useful or usable by the lessor at the end of the lease term and capable of continued leasing or transfer to any party. If such a representation is made, demonstrate its commercial feasibility.

2   Indicate whether the Property would be useful or usable at the end of the lease term by a party other than a member of the Lessee Group, and if so, describe such use.

3   Indicate whether the Property needs to be dismantled, disconnected, or removed from any site on which it was placed or installed in order for possession thereof to be returned to the lessor at the end of the lease term. If so:

(a) Indicate whether and how such dismantling, disconnection, or removal will affect the value of the Property for the purpose for which it was originally intended to be used, and

(b) Demonstrate the commercial feasibility of reassembling, reconnecting or reinstalling the Property at another location.

### .10   Other

1   Set forth the details of the repayment of the portion of the total acquisition cost borrowed by the lessor (debt service), including an analysis of the anticipated repayment of principal and interest on such debt by the lessor.

2   List and explain all provisions of the lease transaction relating to indemnities, termination, obsolescence, casualty, stipulated casualty value, and insurance.

3   State that if the Service rules that the lessor is the owner of the Property for Federal income tax purposes at the time that the Property is first placed in service or use, the lessee will not claim that it is such an owner at such time.

4   State whether the lessor will or will not elect under section 48(d) of the Code to treat the lessee as owner for purposes of the investment tax credit.

### Section 5   Other Instructions

Documents that have been submitted with the request for an advance ruling may, as indicated below, be amended by the parties, prior to the date on which the Property is first placed in service or use. A complete explanation of the changes must be submitted together with specific references to both the original and amended documents. If, as a result of the amended documents, the responses required by section 4 of this Revenue Procedure are modified, the revised responses must be brought to the attention of the Service in such a fashion as to be readily understandable. In situations where the transaction is materially revised by the amendments, the original request for advance ruling, together with all submissions, including the amended documents, will be considered by the Service to be a new request for advance ruling received on the date that it receives the amended documents. The Service ordinarily will not rule on the consequences of a proposed amendment that purports to relate back to the time when the Property was first placed in service or use, or purports to affect the issue of the ownership of the Property at that time.

### Section 6 Effective Date
The provisions of this Revenue Procedure are effective May 6, 1975.

### Section 7 Effect on Other Documents
Rev. Proc 72-3 is modified to the extent provided in section 3.02 of this Revenue Procedure.

### Section 8 Inquiries
Inquiries regarding this Revenue Procedure should refer to its number and be addressed to the Commissioner of Internal Revenue, 1111 Constitution Avenue, N.W., Washington, D.C. 20224, Attention: T:C:C. Rev. Proc 75-28, announced in T. I. R. No. 1371, May 5, 1975, 759 CCH 6573.

### LIMITED USE PROPERTY LEASES—REVENUE PROCEDURE 76-30

The Internal Revenue Service will not issue advance rulings that certain transactions involving leases of so-called limited use property are leases for Federal income tax purposes.

Limited use property is property not expected to be either useful to or usable by a lessor at the end of the lease term except for continued leasing or transfer to a member of the lessee group. The procedure stating the IRS decision contains examples illustrating both the types of property considered to be and not to be limited use property.

### Section 1 Purpose

This Revenue Procedure concerns requests for advance rulings on leveraged lease transactions as described in Rev. Proc. 75-21, 1975-1 C.B. 715, and Rev. Proc. 75-28, 1975-1 C.B. 752. The purpose of this Revenue Procedure is to set forth the decision of the Service not to issue advance rulings that certain transactions purporting to be leases of property are, in fact, leases for Federal income tax purposes when the property is "limited use property."

## Section 2    Background

The Service previously announced in section 5.02 of Rev. Proc. 75-21 that it had not decided whether rulings would be issued in cases involving the leasing of property not expected to be useful to or usable by the lessor at the end of the lease term except for purposes of continued leasing or transfer to a member of the lessee group. Such property is referred to herein as "limited use property."

## Section 3    Decision

Rev. Proc. 75-21 sets forth guidelines relating to advance rulings on leveraged lease transactions. Section 4(1)(C) of those guidelines requires the lessor to represent and demonstrate certain facts relating to the estimated fair market value and estimated remaining useful life of the property at the end of the lease term. This requirement is intended, in part, to assure that the purported lessor has not transferred the use of the property to the purported lessee for substantially its entire useful life. In the case of limited use property, at the end of the lease term there will probably be no potential lessees or buyers other than members of the lessee group. As a result, the lessor of limited use property will probably sell or rent the property to a member of the lessee group, thus enabling the lessee group to enjoy the benefits of the use or ownership of the property for substantially its entire useful life. See Rev. Rul. 55-541, 1955-2 C.B. 19, for an example of a transaction in which property was determined to be leased for substantially its entire useful life and the conclusion that such a transaction transfers equitable ownership. Accordingly, the Service will not issue advance rulings whether certain transactions purporting to be leases of property are, in fact, leases for Federal income tax purposes when the property is limited use property.

## Section 4    Procedure

Pursuant to Rev. Proc. 75-28 taxpayers requesting an advance ruling in a leveraged lease transaction must furnish to the Service certain information and representations. If the information required to be furnished by section 4.09 of Rev. Proc. 75-28 fails to establish that the property is not limited use property, the Service will decline to issue an advance ruling on the transaction. Such information must establish to the satisfaction of the Service that the use of the property at the end of the lease term by the lessor or some person, other than a member of the lessee group, who could lease or purchase the property from the lessor is commercially feasible to the lessor or to both respectively. The Service's determination of commercial feasibility will be based on the standards that would be applied by reasonably prudent businessmen on the basis of present knowledge and generally accepted engineering standards.

## Section 5   Examples

The following examples illustrate the types of property the Service considers to be limited use property, and the types of property the Service does not consider to be limited use property.

1   $X$ builds a masonry smokestack attached to a masonry warehouse building owned by $Y$, and leases the smokestack to $Y$ for use as an addition to the heating system of the warehouse. The lease term is 15 years; the smokestack has a useful life of 25 years, and the warehouse has a remaining useful life of 25 years. It would not be commercially feasible to disassemble the smokestack at the end of the lease term and reconstruct it at a new location. The smokestack is considered to be limited use property.

2   $X$ builds a complete chemical production facility on land owned by $Y$ and leases the facility to $Y$, a manufacturer of chemicals. The lease term is 24 years, and the facility has a useful life of 30 years. The land is leased to $X$ pursuant to a ground lease for a term of 30 years. The technical "know-how" and trade secrets $Y$ possess are necessary elements in the commercial operation of the facility. At the time the lease is entered into no person who is not a member of the lessee group possesses the technical "know-how" and trade secrets necessary for the commercial operation of the facility. The taxpayers submit to the Service the written opinion of a qualified expert stating it is probable that by the expiration of the lease term of the facility third parties who are potential purchasers or lessees of the facility will have independently developed such "know-how" and trade secrets. The facility is considered to be limited use property. In reaching this conclusion, the Service will not take into account such expert opinion because such opinions are too speculative for advance ruling purposes.

3   The facts are the same as in the example set forth in subsection (2) except $X$ has an option, exercisable at the end of the lease term of the facility, to purchase from $Y$ the "know-how" and trade secrets necessary for the commercial operation of the facility, and it would be commercially feasible at the end of such lease term for $X$ to exercise the option and operate the facility itself. The facility is not considered to be limited use property.

4   The facts are the same as in the example set forth in subsection (2) except it would be commercially feasible for the lessor at the end of the lease term to make certain structural modifications of the facility that would make the facility capable of being used by persons not possessing any special technical "know-how" or trade secrets. Furthermore, if such modifications were made, it would be commercially feasible, at the end of the lease term, for a person who is not a member of the lessee group to purchase or lease the facility from $X$. The facility is not considered to be limited use property.

5   $X$ builds an electrical generating plant on land owned by $Y$ and leases the plant to $Y$. The lease term is 40 years, and the plant has an estimated useful life of 50 years. The land is leased to $X$ pursuant to a ground lease for a term of 50

years. The plant is adjacent to a fuel source that it is estimated will last for at least 50 years. Access to this fuel source is necessary for the commercial operation of the plant, and Y has recently obtained the contractual right to acquire all fuel produced from the source for 50 years. Y will use the plant to produce and generate electrical power for sale to a city located 500 miles away. The plant is synchronized into a power grid that makes the sale of electrical power to a number of potential markets commercially feasible. It would not be commercially feasible to disassemble the plant and reconstruct it at a new location. The electrical generating plant is considered to be limited use property because access to this fuel source held exclusively by Y is necessary for the commercial operation of the plant.

6   The facts are the same as in the example set forth in subsection (5) except X has an option, exercisable at the end of the lease term of the plant, to acquire from Y the contractual right to acquire all fuel produced from the fuel source for the 10-year period commencing at the end of such lease term. It would be commercially feasible at the end of such lease term for X to exercise this option. Furthermore, it would be commercially feasible, at the end of such lease term, for a person who is not a member of the lessee group to purchase the contractual right to the fuel from X for an amount equal to the option price and purchase or lease the plant from X. The plant is not considered to be limited use property.

## Section 6   Effect on Other Documents

Rev. Proc. 75-21 is modified.

## Section 7   Inquiries

Inquiries in regard to this Revenue Procedure should refer to its number and be addressed to the Commissioner of Internal Revenue, Attention T:C:C, 1111 Constitution Avenue, N.W., Washington, D.C. 20224. Rev. Proc. 76-30, 1976-2 C.B. 647.

*Chapter 4*

# LEGAL ASPECTS
# OF LEASE FINANCING

From a legal perspective, lease financing can be divided into three major categories: (1) sale-leasebacks of real property (e.g., land and/or buildings or parts of buildings); (2) chattel leases intended as security agreements (e.g., leases of equipment, aircraft, computers); (3) true leases of personal property. There is a fourth category of lease that involves the right to exploit real property through mining, drilling for oil or gas, or recovery of other natural resources. Such leases are beyond the scope of this book. This chapter will concentrate primarily on sale-leasebacks of real property.

## LEASES OF REAL PROPERTY

Rights of ownership in real property are called estates and are classified to indicate the quantity, nature, and extent of the rights. The two major categories of estates are freehold estates (those existing for an indefinite time) and estates that are less than freehold (those that exist for a predetermined time).

Estates less than freehold, often called leasehold estates, are discussed in general terms as follows.

A real property lease is both a contract and a grant of an estate in real property. A lease is a contract by which the owner of the real property, the landlord (lessor), grants to another, the tenant (lessee), an exclusive right to the use and possession of the real property for a definite or ascertainable period of time. The time of possession is called the lease term. The principal characteristics of the lease estate are that it continues for a definite or ascertainable term and that it carries with it the obligation on the part of the lessee to pay rent to the lessor.

By law, in most states, leases for a term longer than a specified period of time must be in writing. The period is fixed at 1 year in some states; in others, it is 3 years. A copy of a lease contract appears at the end of this chapter.

## Lessee's Obligation to Pay Rent

Although the leasehold estate carries with it an implied obligation to pay reasonable rent, the lease contract almost always contains an express promise, known as a convenant, by the lessee to pay rent in specified amounts at specified times. There are several reasons for this. The most obvious is that, in the absence of such an express convenant providing the amount of rental and the times for payment, the rent is stipulated to be a reasonable amount and is payable only at the end of the term.

Aside from the economic advantage of setting the amount of the rent without recourse to the courts and of obtaining payment in stated installments, the lessee's express covenant to pay rent serves other useful functions.

Most leases contain a provision to the effect that breach by the lessee of any of his covenants in the lease will entitle the lessor to declare the lease at an end, and will give him the right to regain possession of the property. The lessee's express undertaking to pay rent thus becomes one of the covenants on which this provision can operate. Under the common law, if there were no such provision in the lease, the lessee's failure to pay rent when due would give the lessor only the right to recover a judgment for the amount of such rent; it would give him no right to evict the lessee from the premises or to regain the property. This is a direct result of the common-law doctrine that the mutual covenants in a lease are independent of one another, unless the lease contains an express provision to the contrary. If the lessee breaches his covenant to pay rent, or fails to perform any of the other covenants in the lease, the lessor is not relieved of his covenant to provide the lessee with quiet enjoyment of the property. Although the lessor could successfully sue the lessee for breach of contract, he could not treat that breach as an excuse for nonperformance by the lessor.

In many states today, the common-law rule has been changed by statute so that the lessor is given a right to dispossess the lessee for nonpayment of rent although there is no provision for this in the lease. However, such statutes give the lessor a meaningful remedy only where the lease contains an express covenant to pay rent in stated installments or in advance. Rent that is not expressly made payable in advance or in stated installments becomes payable only at the end of the term.

## Termination of the Lessee's Obligation to Pay Rent

The implied obligation to pay reasonable rent, because it arises out of the leasehold, ceases when the leasehold is transferred by assignment. Thus when the lessee assigns a lease that does not contain an express agreement to pay rent, the implied obligation to pay reasonable rent passes to the assignee. This is not true where the lease contains an express agreement of the lessee to pay rent. Under an express covenant to pay rent, the lessee remains liable despite the fact that he has assigned the leasehold to another lessee, unless the lessor releases him from the obligation. The assignee is also liable to the lessor for the stipulated rent. The assignee of a lease that contains an express covenant to pay rent is liable for the stipulated rent—not for the reasonable rent. This result is derived from the theory that certain covenants in the lease, of which the covenant to pay rent is one, run with the property. Such covenants pass to the assignee of the lease as if they were attached to the property covered by the lease. Covenants that have this quality of "running with the land" are covenants that "touch and concern" the land and thus "run" with it: covenants to pay rent, covenants to pay taxes, options to renew, options to purchase, covenants to repair and restore, and covenants to keep the premises insured.

Under this doctrine, the covenant to pay rent passes to the assignee of the lease as long as he remains in possession of the property. Although the assignee of the lease is thus bound to pay rent, the original lessee is not relieved of his contractual obligation to pay rent. Should the assignee fail to pay the stipulated rent, the original lessee will have to pay it. He will, of course, have a right to be reimbursed by the assignee.

Without specific restrictions in the lease, leases are freely assignable. Many leases, however, prohibit assignment without the lessor's written consent. If the lessee assigns without written consent, the assignment is not void, but it may be ignored by the lessor. In other words, the prohibition of assignment in a lease is only for the benefit of the lessor and cannot be relied on by the assignor to terminate an otherwise valid assignment on the grounds that the lessor did not consent. If, however, the lessor accepts rent from the assignee, he will be held to have waived the restriction. The restriction, once waived, cannot be revived by the lessor on subsequent assignments.

A sublease differs from an assignment in that it involves the transfer, by one lessee to another, of less than all the lessee's rights in the lease. For example, Hero Manufacturing is a lessee under a lease that is to terminate on December 31, 1981. Hero enters into an agreement with Xenon Electronics that is called "Assignment of Lease." The agreement provides that Hero "hereby assigns all its right, title, and interest in the above lease to" Xenon Electronics, for a stated sum of money, and provides further that if Xenon Electronics does not pay the rent stipulated in the lease to Hero's lessor, "then and in that event Hero reserves the right to reenter the said premises." Most courts say that even though this agreement is labeled "Assignment of Lease," Hero has not, in fact, assigned the lease but has merely subleased. The reason is that Hero has reserved a right of reentry, that is, it has in fact transferred less than its whole interest in the lease. Most subleases are easily recognizable as such. The typical sublease would arise in the foregoing example if Hero leased the premises to Xenon for a shorter period than that covered by its own lease, for example, until December 30, 1980, at a stated rental payable to Hero rather than to Hero's landlord.

The legal effects of a sublease are different from those of an assignment. In a sublease, the sublessee, Xenon in the example, has no obligation to the lessor. Xenon's obligations run solely to Hero, the original lessee. Hero is not relieved of any of its obligations under the lease. The doctrine that certain covenants run with the property has no application to a sublease. Thus the lessor has no right of action against Hero's sublessee Xenon, under any covenants contained in the original lease between it and Hero, because that lease has not been assigned to Xenon. Hero, of course, remains liable for the rent stipulated and for all the other covenants of the lessee in the original lease between it and the lessor.

## Effects of Destruction of the Property on the Lessee's Obligation to Pay Rent

The dual character of a lease as a contract and as a grant of an estate in land is demonstrated when we consider the common-law rule governing the destruction of the property by fire or other fortuitous cause.

Where the lessee leases land together with a building and the building is destroyed by fire or some other fortuitous cause, the common law does not relieve the lessee of its obligation to pay rent nor does it permit the lessee to terminate the lease. The reason for this rule is that the common law regards the lessee's obligation to pay rent as given in exchange for the estate in the land. The concept of an estate at common law is divorced from the economic benefits that go with it. Thus although the destruction of a building may very well deprive the lessee of the entire economic benefit of the lease, the common law does not permit the lessee to argue that the destruction of the building in fact amounted to a destruction of the estate.

The common-law rule has been modified in some states by statute, for example, New York Real Property Law 227, and in most states it is not applied to lessees who occupy only a portion of the building and have no interest in the building as a whole, for example, office lessees. Most courts take the view that it would be stretching the concept of an estate too far to say that a lessee occupying a few floors in a building is left with his estate, in return for which he must pay rent, despite the total destruction of the building.

Most leases contain clauses covering the fortuitous destruction of the premises. A typical cause provides that, on damage by fire or other fortuitous cause, the lessor will repair and restore and that if the premises are wholly unusable the lessee's obligation to pay rent will be suspended until the premises are restored, but that if the lessor decides to demolish and reconstruct the premises the lease will terminate.

This standard clause has several disadvantages to the business tenant. If the landlord elects to repair, the tenant remains bound under the lease although his business may be suspended long enough to cause a substantial loss of profit. Moreover, the tenant remains liable for the full rent if the premises, though partially destroyed, are not "wholly untenantable." In a sale and leaseback and other types of lease financing, this clause is usually modified to stipulate that the lessee will repurchase the property for, or pay to the lessor, a specified casualty value in the event of destruction of the property.

## Effect of Public Controls and Condemnation on Lessee's Obligation to Pay Rent

A lessee proposing to make a particular business use of the property should be careful to check the applicable zoning ordinances before it enters into a lease. An existing zoning ordinance prohibiting the use that the lessee has in mind when it enters into the lease will not relieve the lessee of the obligation to pay rent. An exception may be made, however, in the case where the lease specifically restricts the lessee's use to a use that subsequently becomes outlawed by a zoning ordinance. In such cases, the concept of commercial frustration may be applied by the courts to relieve the lessee of its obligations under the lease. It has been held that an existing zoning restriction, prohibiting the use to which the property was expressly limited under the terms of the lease, does not relieve the lessee of its obligations under the lease.

Total condemnation of the property for public use may cause termination of the lease and relieve the lessee from obligations under it. Partial condemnation, however, does not relieve the lessee from its obligation to pay rent. For example, where Exciting Films Corp. leases an office building for 5 years, and in the first year a portion of the building is condemned for the construction of a road, Exciting Films must continue to pay full rent to the lessor for the remainder of the term. The lessee is entitled, however, to as much of the condemnation award as represents the rent it would be required to pay to the lessor for the portion of the building condemned for the remainder of the term. Because this computation has the tendency to exhaust a substantial portion of the condemnation award, lessors prefer to insert a clause in the lease providing for a proportionate reduction of the rent, reserving to themselves the right to claim the entire condemnation award.

*Abandonment by Lessee* If the lessee wrongfully abandons the property before the expiration of the term of the lease and the lessor reenters the property or re-leases it to another, the courts have held that the lessee's obligation to pay rent terminates. The lessor, if it desires to hold the lessee to its obligation to pay rent, must either leave the property vacant, or it must have available in the lease a "survival clause" covering this situation. Such survival clauses generally provide that, on wrongful abandonment by the lessee, the lessor may re-lease the property "as agent for the lessee" and that the lessee will remain liable to the lessor for the difference between the rent stipulated in the lease and the rent obtained on such re-lease minus costs of re-leasing. Under such a clause, the lessee remains liable for the rent, the lease is not terminated as in the case of eviction, and the lessor may sue the lessee on the dates when installments of rent become due and payable under the original lease.

*The Obligation to Repair and Restore*    The lessee is under no duty to make any repairs to the property, unless the lease expressly provides. The lessee is not obliged to repair or restore substantial or extraordinary damage occurring with its fault or to repair damage caused by ordinary wear and tear. If damage occurs, the lessee continues to pay rent and to enjoy the use of the unrepaired premises. However, in sale-leasebacks of real property, where the transaction is, in reality, a means of financing the property for the lessee, the lessee ordinarily desires to keep the property in good working order.

The lessor, likewise, is under no duty to repair and maintain premises that it has wholly leased to another, unless the lease expressly so provides. However, the lessor is under a duty to repair and maintain any portion of the premises that remain under his control. For example, a building owner who controls the stairways, elevators, and other common areas is liable for their maintenance and repair and is responsible for injuries occurring as a result of his failure to do so. In respect to buildings, the presumption is that any portion of the property that is not expressly leased to the lessee remains under the lessor's control. Thus the lessor in such cases is liable to make external repairs, including repairs to the roof.

The obligations to repair and to restore the premises are usually covered by the provisions of the lease. A lessee's covenant to repair has been interpreted by the courts as including an obligation to restore the premises after destruction by fire or other fortuitous cause. The same result has been reached in the case of the lessor's covenant to repair. A lessee or lessor who does not wish to undertake such a duty should be careful to qualify his duty to repair with the clause "reasonable wear and tear or damage by the elements excepted." Care should be taken to avoid ambiguity on this point. Failure to do so may present the situation of a lease that contains a standard clause dealing with destruction by fire or other fortuitous cause, coupled with a provision requiring the lessee to repair, and ending with a clause "at the expiration of this lease the tenant shall return the premises in as good condition as they now are, reasonable wear and tear or damage by the elements excepted." Although the standard clause dealing with destruction by fire requiring the lessor to restore is not inconsistent with the final clause, the clause requiring the lessee to "repair" without qualification is obviously inconsistent with the other two.

*Indemnification Clauses*   The majority of leases contain an exculpation or indemnification clause by which either the lessor or lessee or both attempt to limit their liability for damages for injuries to persons or property caused by their own negligence. Exculpation excuses one party from liability for otherwise valid claims that may be made against them by the other party to the lease. Indemnification represents a promise by one party that the other party will be secure from loss or damage from claims made by a third person. Some states prohibit exculpation clauses excusing a lessor from liability for its own negligence. Where a lessor seeks protection by indemnification from a lessee, the lessee may limit its exposure by obtaining liability insurance. Sale-leasebacks also frequently have tax indemnification clauses. A tax indemnification clause states that the lessee will indemnify the lessor if for some reason the IRS does not recognize the transaction as a valid sale and a true lease.

## Expiration of the Lease

A lease for a definite term expires at the end of the term by virtue of its own limitation. Most lease financing agreements are for a definite term.

A periodic tenancy is a definite term to be held over and over in indefinite succession. To illustrate, a lease "to A from month to month" or "from year to year" creates a periodic tenancy. A periodic tenancy may be terminated by either party at the expiration of any one period but only after giving adequate notice to the other party.

A lease containing a provision that either party may terminate at will creates a tenancy at will. So does a lease that does not specify any duration.

## SALE-LEASEBACKS OF REAL ESTATE

A sale and leaseback involves a valid contract of sale and a valid real property lease. Since the true intention of the parties in a sale and leaseback of real estate is often to place themselves in the same position they would have been in had they entered a mortgage loan arrangement, the lease contract should be oriented to:

1  Protecting the ability of the lessee to use and enjoy the property in the same manner as if he were the owner.
2  Protecting the principal amount of sums advanced to the lessee (the sales price).
3  Protecting the interest payments on the principal amount (the lease payments less the return of principal).
4  Protecting the tax position of the lessor.

The following is an example of a typical contract in a sale and leaseback arrangement of real property.

## TABLE OF CONTENTS

LEASE AGREEMENT, dated as of May 15, 1980 between _____
, a _____corporation having an office at _____
_____(the "Lessor"), and _____
_____, a _____cor-
poration having an office at _____(the "Lessee").

## WITNESSETH:

## ARTICLE I

**Certain Definitions**

Section 1.1. As used in this Lease:

"Assignment" means the Present Assignment of Rents dated as of May 15, 1980, from the Lessor and the Lessee to the Trustees, as the same may at any time be supplemented or amended, pursuant to which the Lessor assigns to the Trustees all sums then due and thereafter becoming due to the Lessor under this Lease.

"Improvements" means all buildings and other improvements now located or hereafter erected upon the Land, together with all machinery, apparatus, equipment, fittings, fixtures, and articles of personal property now or hereafter attached to or used in connection with the same, and all additions to and replacements or substitutions of any thereof.

"Indenture" means the Indenture dated as of May 15, 1980 between the Company and _____and _____ , as Trustees, as the same may at any time be supplemented or amended.

"Land" means the real property located in _____ more particularly described as Parcel 1 in Schedule I hereto.

"Notes" means the 11 $\frac{1}{2}$ percent Notes and any Improvement Notes (as such terms are defined in the Indenture) issued under and secured by the Indenture.

"Permitted Encumbrances" means (a) the Indenture; (b) this Lease; (c) the Assignment; (d) Liens for Impositions which are not due and delinquent or which can be paid without penalty; (e) Liens, the validity, applicability, or amount of which is being contested in good faith by appropriate proceedings in accordance with Article VIII; and (f) other minor and immaterial liens, charges, or encumbrances which do not and will not interfere with the use of the Property by the Lessor or the Lessee in the normal conduct of their respective businesses and which do not materially impair the value of the Property.

"Property" means, collectively, the Land and the Improvements.

"Trustee" means, collectively, _____and ____ and their successors in trust and assigns, as Trustees under the Indenture.

"Unavoidable Delays" means delays due to strikes, acts of God or the public enemy, governmental restrictions, civil commotion, vandalism, fire, casualty or other causes, similar or dissimilar, beyond the control of the Lessee.


## ARTICLE II

### Premises—Term—Renewal Terms

Section 2.1. In consideration of and subject to the rents, covenants, and agreements hereinafter set forth, the Lessor hereby demises and leases to the Lessee, and the Lessee hereby takes and hires from the Lessor the Property, together with all privileges, easements, franchises, rights, and appurtenances of whatsoever kind relating thereto, including, without limitation, the privileges, easements, franchises, rights, and appurtenances described in Parcel 2 of Schedule I hereto.

TO HAVE AND TO HOLD the Property unto the Lessee, its successors and assigns, for an interim term of 3 days, commencing on May 28, 1980 and ending on May 31, 1980 (the "Interim Term") and for a basic term of 30 years commencing on June 1, 1980 and ending on May 31, 2010 (the "Basic Term").

Section 2.2. The Lessee represents and warrants that (a) it has caused good and marketable title to the Property to be conveyed to the Lessor, free and clear of all liens, charges, and encumbrances except Permitted Encumbrances, and (b) failure of title through any defect existing at such time including title paramount, shall not release the Lessee from any of its obligations hereunder.

Section 2.3. If no Event of Default (as hereinafter defined) shall have occurred and be continuing, the Lessee shall have the right to renew the term of this Lease, for three successive periods of 17 years each, by giving the Lessor notice of its election to renew not less than 6 months prior to the expiration of the Basic Term or of the then current renewal term, as the case may be, each renewal term to be upon the same terms, convenants, and conditions as in this Lease provided, except that (a) there shall be no right to renew the term of this Lease for any period of time beyond the expiration of the last renewal term and (b) the annual basic rent shall be $204,050 during the first renewal term and $174,900 during each successive renewal term, payable in each case in equal quarterly installments in advance.

## ARTICLE III

### Rent

Section 3.1. The Lessee shall pay to the Lessor during the Interim Term an interim rental (the "Interim Rent") of $6801.67, payable on June 1, 1980, and during the Basic Term an annual basic rent (the "Basic Rent") of $624,908.04, payable in advance in equal quarterly installments of $156,227.01 each on the first days of March, June, September, and December in each year commencing on June 1, 1980 and ending on March 1, 2010.

Section 3.2. If any installment of Interim Rent or Basic Rent shall not be paid when due, the Lessee, to the extent permitted by applicable law, shall pay to the Lessor, on demand, interest on the amount of such overdue installment at the rate of 11 ½ percent per annum from the date the same is due.

Section 3.3. This Lease shall be completely net to the Lessor and the Interim Rent, the Basic Rent, and the Additional Rent (as hereinafter defined) shall be paid to the Lessor at the address of the Lessor set forth above, or at such other address as the Lessor shall designate to the Lessee in writing, in lawful money of the United States, in immediately available funds at the place of payment, without notice or demand and without abatement, deduction, or set-off of any amount whatsoever.

Section 3.4. The Lessor hereby grants to the Lessee a partial abatement of Interim Rent and Basic Rent in the amount of $349,800 to be credited against the first installments of Interim Rent and Basic Rent payable hereunder.

Section 3.5. At any one time during the eleventh through the twentieth years of the Basic Term, the Lessee may request the Lessor to refinance the Notes at a rate and on terms not to exceed such maximum limits as the Lessee shall specify in such request. The Lessor shall use its best efforts to accomplish such refinancing within 6 months after such request or prior to the end of the twentieth year of the Basic Term, whichever is earlier. All costs of such refinancing, including, without limitation, any premium payable on the prepayment of the Notes, shall be borne by the Lessee. In the event such refinancing is carried out, the annual Basic Rent during the remainder of the Basic Term shall be reduced by 50 percent of the amount by which the annual debt service on the Notes shall have been reduced as a result of such refinancing, and the Lessor and the Lessee shall execute and deliver all such documents and instruments as may be required by the lender and its counsel, in form and substance satisfactory to the lender and its counsel, to accomplish such refinancing, including, but not limited to, an amendment to this Lease, a note, a mortgage, and an assignment of this Lease.

## ARTICLE IV

### Impositions

Section 4.1. Subject to Article VIII, the Lessee shall pay, before any fine, penalty, interest, or cost attaches thereto, all taxes, assessments, water and sewer rates, and all other governmental charges or levies now or hereafter assessed, levied, confirmed, imposed or which become a lien upon, or which become payable in respect of, any part of the Property during the term of this Lease (collectively, "Impositions"), and shall furnish to the Lessor, upon request, official receipts or other satisfactory evidence of payment of the same; provided, however, that if by law any Imposition may be paid in installments (whether or not interest shall accrue on the unpaid balance thereof), the Lessee may pay such Imposition (together with accrued interest on the unpaid balance thereof) in installments as the same respectively become due and before any fine, penalty, interest, or cost attaches thereto; and provided, further, that any imposition relating to a fiscal year of the taxing authority, a part of which period is included within the term of this Lease and a part of which is included in a period of time after the termination of this Lease (other than a termination pursuant to Article XVII), shall (whether or not such Imposition shall be assessed, levied, confirmed, imposed or become a lien upon or become payable in respect of the Property during the term of this Lease) be adjusted between the Lessor and the Lessee as of the termination of this Lease, so that the Lessor shall pay that portion of such Imposition which that part of such fiscal period included in the period of time after the termination of this Lease bears to such fiscal period, and the Lessee shall pay the remainder thereof.

Section 4.2. The certificate, advice, or bill of the appropriate official designated by law to make or issue the same or to receive payment of any Imposition showing nonpayment of any Imposition shall be prima facie evidence that such imposition is due and unpaid at the time of the making or issuance of such certificate, advice, or bill.


## ARTICLE V

### Insurance

Section 5.1. The Lessee shall at all times maintain insurance for the mutual benefit of the Lessor and the Lessee against:

**(a)** loss or damage to the Improvements by fire and such other risks as may be included in the standard form of extended coverage endorsement from time to time available in amounts sufficient to prevent the Lessor or the Lessee from becoming a co-insurer under the terms of the applicable policies but, in any event, in an amount not less than 80 percent of the full insurable value of the Improvements as determined from time to time;

**(b)** claims for personal injury or property damage occurring in or about the Property, under a policy of general public liability insurance, with such limits as may reasonable be required by the Lessor from time to time, but not less than $500,000 in respect of bodily injury to or death of any one person and not less than $1,000,000 in respect of bodily injury to or death of any number of persons in any one occurrence and not less than $100,000 in respect of property damage; and

**(c)** such other hazards and in such amounts as the Lessor may reasonably require, provided such insurance is customarily maintained for Improvements of similar construction, use and class.

The term "full insurable value" shall mean actual replacement cost (exclusive of cost of excavation, foundations, and footings below the basement floor) without deduction for physical depreciation. All such insurance required to be maintained by this Article shall be issued by financially responsible insurers authorized to do business in the State in which the Property is located.

Section 5.2. All insurance policies maintained by the Lessee pursuant to Section 5.1 shall name the Lessor, the Lessee, and the Trustee as the insureds as their respective interests may appear, and shall bear a standard noncontributory first mortgagee endorsement substantially equivalent to the New York standard mortgagee endorsement in favor of the Trustee. Such insurance shall provide that (a) all property losses insured against shall be adjusted by the Lessee (subject to the Lessor's approval of final settlement of estimated losses of $50,000 or more) and that the proceeds thereof in excess of $50,000 shall be paid to the Trustee or, if there be none, to the Lessor, to be applied in the manner set forth in Article XVI, (b) no cancellation or reduction thereof shall be effective until at least 10 days after receipt by the Lessor and the Trustee of notice thereof, and (c) all losses shall be payable nothwithstanding (i) any act or negligence of the Lessor, the Lessee or the Trustee or their respective agents or employees which might, absent such agreement, result in a forfeiture of all or part of such insurance payment, (ii) the occupation or use of the Property for purposes more hazardous than permitted by the terms of such policy, (iii) any foreclosure or other action or proceeding taken pursuant to any provision of the Indenture on the happening of an event of default thereunder, or (iv) any change in title or ownership of the Property or any part thereof. Such insurance may provide for deductible amounts of not more than $50,000. The Lessee shall on the execution hereof furnish to the Lessor and the Trustee originals of such policies or certificates therefor and, not less than 30 days before the expiration of any such insurance, policies or certificates evidencing the replacement or renewal thereof, together with written evidence that the premium has been paid and a certificate of the insurer or of an independent insurance underwriter of recognized standing to the effect that such insurance complies with all of the requirements of this Article.

Section 5.3. Any loss paid under any such insurance policies to the Trustee or the Lessor shall be held by the Trustee or the Lessor, as the case may be, as a trust fund to be paid to or for the account of the Lessee in accordance with the provisions of Article XVI for application to the cost of restoring, repairing, replacing, or rebuilding the Improvements, except as provided in Section 14.2.

Section 5.4. Nothing contained in this Article shall prevent the Lessee from maintaining or causing to be maintained insurance against the risks referred to in Section 5.1 under a policy or policies of blanket insurance, which may cover other properties owned by the Lessee as well as the Property, provided, however, that any such policy of blanket insurance:

(a)   shall specify therein, or the Lessee shall furnish the Lessor and the Trustee with a written statement from the insurers under such policies specifying, the amount of the total insurance allocated to each of the Improvements included inthe Property, which amount shall not be less than the amount required by Section 5.1 to be carried;

(b)   shall not contain any clause which would result in the insured thereunder being required to carry insurance with respect to the property covered thereby in an amount not less than any specific percentage of the full insurable value of such property in order to prevent the insured therein named from becoming a co-insurer of any loss with the insurer under such policy; and

**(c)**   shall in all other respects comply with the other provisions of Section 5.1.

Section 5.5. The Lessee shall not take out separate insurance with respect to the Improvements concurrent in form or contributing in the event of loss with that required by this Article unless the same shall contain a standard noncontributory first mortgage endorsement substantially equivalent to the New York standard mortgagee endorsement with loss payable to the Trustee.

## ARTICLE VI

### Compliance with Laws

Section 6.1. Subject to Article VIII, the Lessee shall comply with all laws and ordinances and the orders and requirements of all Federal, state, and municipal governments and the appropriate departments, commissions, boards, and officers thereof, and the orders, rules, and regulations of the Board of Fire Underwriters or any other body hereafer constituted exercising similar functions, which at any time may be applicable to the Property (collectively, "Legal Requirements"), whether or not compliance therewith shall necessitate changes to the Improvements, interior or exterior, structural or otherwise, or interfere with the use and enjoyment of the Property or any part thereof.

Section 6.2. The Lessee shall procure, maintain, and comply with all permits, licenses, and other authorizations required for any use of the Property or any part thereof.

## ARTICLE VII

### Liens

Section 7.1. Subject to Article VIII, the Lessee shall not create, suffer to exist, or permit any mortgage, lien, charge, or encumbrance (collectively "Liens") to be filed against the Property or any part thereof or against the Lessee's leasehold estate therein, except Permitted Encumbrances. Without limiting the generality of the foregoing the Lessee shall post a notice or notices in accordance with the Provisions of §61-2-10, New Mexico Statutes Annotated, or the corresponding provision of any similar law hereafter in effect to assure that no Lien shall be filed against the Lessor or its interest in the Property.

Section 7.2. Nothing in this Lease contained shall be deemed or construed in any way as constituting the consent of or request by the Lessor, express or implied, to any contractor, subcontractor, laborer, or materialman for the performance of any labor or the furnishing of any meterials for any specific improvement, alteration to or repair of the Property or any part thereof, nor as giving the Lessee a right, power, or authority to contract for or permit the rendering of any services or the furnishing of any materials that would give rise to the filing of any such lien against the Property or any part thereof or against the Lessee's leasehold estate therein.

## ARTICLE VIII

### Permitted Contests

Section 8.1. The Lessee may contest, by appropriate legal proceedings conducted in good faith and with due diligence, the amount or validity or application, in whole or in part, of any Impositions, Legal Requirements, or Liens provided that (a) in the case of unpaid Impositions or Liens, the commencement and continuation of such proceedings shall suspend the collection thereof from the Lessor and the Property, (b) neither the Property nor any rent therefrom nor any part thereof or interest therein would be in any danger of being sold, forfeited, attached, or lost, (c) in the case of Legal Requirements, the Lessor would not be in any danger of civil or criminal liability for failure to comply therewith pending the outcome of such proceedings, and (d) the Lessee shall have furnished such security, if any, as may be required in the proceedings or as the Lessor may reasonably require to assure the discharge of such Impositions or Liens or compliance with such Legal Requirements on the termination of such proceedings.

Section 8.2. The Lessor shall execute and deliver to the Lessee such authorizations and other documents as may reasonably be required in any such proceedings and, if reasonably requested by the Lessee, shall join as a party therein. The Lessee shall indemnify and save the Lessor harmless against any cost or expense of any kind that may be imposed on the Lessor in connection with any such proceedings and any loss resulting therefrom.

## ARTICLE IX

### Utilities

Section 9.1. The lessee shall pay or cause to be paid all charges or taxes for heat, water and sewer, gas, electricity, light, telephone, or any other communication or utility service used in or rendered or supplied to the Property or any part thereof.

## ARTICLE X

### Repairs and Maintenance

Section 10.1. The Lessee shall take good care of the Property and shall keep and maintain the same, and the adjoining sidewalks, in a clean and orderly condition, free of accumulation of dirt, rubbish, snow, and ice. The Lessee shall not cause or permit any waste, damage, or injury to the Property or any part thereof.

Section 10.2. The Lessee shall promptly make all repairs and replacements to the Property, interior and exterior, structural and otherwise, ordinary and extraordinary, foreseen and unforeseen. All repairs shall, to the extent possible, be at least equivalent in quality to the original work. The Lessee hereby waives the right to make repairs at the expense of the Lessor pursuant to any law in effect at the time of the execution of this Lease or hereafter enacted.

## ARTICLE XI

### Changes and Alterations—Surrender of Property

Section 11.1. The Lessee shall have the right, at any time and from time to time, to make such changes, alterations, additions, or improvements (collectively, "Alterations"), structural or otherwise, to the Improvements included in the Property as the lessee shall deem necessary or desirable, provided that all work done in connection with any such Alteration shall be done in compliance with all Legal Requirements, and provided, further, that any such Alteration not change the general characteristics of the Property and shall be of such character that, when completed, the fair market value of the Property shall not be less than the fair market value of the Property immediately before such Alteration.

Section 11.2. (a) If the cost to the Lessee of making all such Alterations to the Property which are completed during any period of 24 consecutive months shall exceed in the aggregate $500,000, then, within 6 months after the expiration of such 24 month period, the Lessee may request the Lessor to finance such cost (which cost for the purposes of this Section 11.2 may include, in addition to the actual cost of construction, the fees and disbursements of architects, engineers and counsel; interest on indebtedness; duplication or printing expenses; filing, registration, and recording fees and taxes; commitment fees; financing fees and expenses; cost of insurance for additions or improvements; and title insurance premiums and documentary stamp taxes). Such request shall (a) describe such Alterations in reasonable detail and state the dates on which the same were completed and (b) certify in reasonable detail the cost of each such Alteration.

(b) Within 30 days after receipt by the Lessor of such request, the Lessor and the Lessee shall enter into good faith negotiations toward an agreement as to what are reasonable terms upon which financing may be carried out, based upon mutually determined reasonable money costs under then existing market conditions. The Lessor shall accept or equal any financing which may be arranged by or offered through the efforts of the Lessee, provided that such financing is consistent with the applicable terms of the Indenture. The Lessee shall execute and deliver in connection with any such financing all such supplements to this Lease (which shall, among other things, increase the Basic Rent and purchase prices payable hereunder by the Lessee by amounts sufficient to assure to the lenders providing such financing the payment of all interest and principal due thereon during the term of this Lease in effect at the time such financing is carried out and appropriately increase on Schedule II hereto the Capitalized Cost of the Property) and cause to be furnished such other opinions and documents including, without limitation, evidence of title insurance, as may be necessary to enable the Lessor to effect such financing under the terms of this Indenture or otherwise which may be required by any such lenders.

(c) If such financing is carried out, the Lessor shall pay to the Lessee the amount of the cost of such Alterations to the extent of the proceeds of such financing. If for any reason such financing is not carried out, the Lessee may offer to purchase the Property in accordance with the provisions of Article XXI at the purchase price calculated in Schedule II hereto.

Section 11.3. The Lessee shall have the right to erect, install, maintain, and operate on the Property such equipment, trade and business fixtures, and signs as the Lessee may deem necessary or desirable provided the same are installed in accordance with all Legal Requirements and all necessary permits and variances are obtained by the Lessee.

Section 11.4. All Alterations and all building service equipment, made or installed by or on behalf of the Lessee (other than equipment, movable trade fixtures, furniture, furnishings, and signs), shall immediately upon completion or installation thereof be and become the property of the Lessor without payment therefor by the lessor.

Section 11.5. The Lessee shall, upon the expiration or earlier termination of this Lease, surrender the Property to the Lessor together with all Alterations thereto and replacements thereof, in good order and condition, except for reasonable wear and tear or damage by fire or other cause. The Lessee shall be entitled to remove equipment, movable trade fixtures, furniture, furnishings, and signs during the term of this Lease or upon expiration of the same or, if the term shall end prior to the date herein specifically fixed for such expiration, then within a period not exceeding 30 days thereafter and upon the expiration or earlier termination of this Lease, if the Lessor so requests, the Lessee shall be obligated to so remove the same; the Lessee to repair any and all damage to the Property resulting from or caused by such removal.

# ARTICLE

## Inspection by Lessor and Trustee

Section 12.1 The Lessor and the Trustee, and their authorized representatives, shall have the right to enter and inspect the Property at all reasonable times during normal business hours, provided such entry shall not unreasonably interfere with the conduct of the Lessee's business thereon.

# ARTICLE XIII

## Lessor's Right to Perform Lessee's Convenants

Section 13.1. If the Lessee shall at any time fail to make any payment or perform any other act on its part to be made or performed under this Lease, the Lessor, after not less than 30 days' notice to the Lessee (except in case of emergency) may, but shall not be obligated to, make such payment or perform such other act to the extent the Lessor may deem desirable, and in connection therewith pay expenses and employ counsel. All such sums and expenses paid by the Lessor shall be deemed to be Additional Rent hereunder (the "Additional Rent") and shall be payable to the Lessor on the first day of the next succeeding month, together with interest thereon at the rate of 11 ½ percent per annum from the date such sums or expenses were paid by the Lessor. In the event of the failure of the Lessee to pay the same, the Lessor shall have the same rights and remedies for the nonpayment thereof as in the case of default in the payment of Basic Rent.

# ARTICLE XIV

## Damage to or Destruction of Improvements

Section 14.1. In case of damage to or destruction of the Improvements included in the Property by fire or otherwise, the Lessee shall promptly give notice thereof to the Lessor and restore, repair, replace, or rebuild the same as nearly as possible to the value and condition thereof immediately prior to such damage or destruction, without abatement, deduction, or set-off of any Interim Rent, Basic Rent, or Additional Rent or any other amount required to be paid by the Lessee hereunder whatsoever. Such restoration, repairs, replacements, or rebuilding shall be commenced promptly and prosecuted with reasonable diligence, subject to Unavoidable Delays.

Section 14.2. If the Improvements included in the Property shall be substantially damaged or destroyed by fire or otherwise, the Lessee, in lieu of restoring, repairing, replacing, or rebuilding the same in accordance with the provisions of Section 14.1, may offer to purchase the Property (and the Lessor's interest in any proceeds of insurance) in accordance with the provisions of Article XXI at the purchase price calculated in Schedule II hereto. If such purchase is consummated, the Lessor, simultaneously with such purchase, shall assign all insurance proceeds relating to the Property to the Lessee. If for any reason said purchase is not consummated, the Lessor shall be entitled to retain any such insurance proceeds and the Lessee shall pay to the Lessor the amount of any loss not reimbursed by such insurance. The Improvements included in the Property shall be deemed to be "substantially damaged or destroyed" if the Lessee determines that such Improvements cannot reasonably be restored, repaired, replaced, or rebuilt as nearly as possible to the value and condition thereof immediately prior to such damage or destruction within 1 year after such damage or destruction.

## ARTICLE XV

### Condemnation

Section 15.1. If all or any part of the Property shall be taken as a result of the exercise of the power of eminent domain (the "proceeding"), the Lessor shall be entitled to receive the award or awards for such taking, to be applied in accordance with the provisions of Article XVI, except as hereinafter provided.

Section 15.2. If the entire Property shall be taken in any such proceeding the Lessee shall, or, in the case of a taking of less than the entire Property, if the Lessee shall determine that the remaining portion of the Property cannot be so repaired or restored that the same can be effectively used in the conduct of the Lessee's business thereon, the Lessee may offer to purchase the Property (and the Lessor's interest in any award arising out of such proceeding) in accordance with the provisions of Article XXI at the purchase price calculated in Schedule II hereto. If such purchase is consummated, the Lessor, simultaneously with such purchase, shall assign all right, title, and interest it may have in and to any such award arising out of such proceeding to the Lessee. If for any reason such purchase is not consummated, the Lessor shall be entitled to retain any such award.

Section 15.3. If less than the entire Property shall be taken in any such proceeding and the Property is not purchased in accordance with the provisions of Article XXI as in Section 15.2 provided, the Lessee shall, as promptly as possible, subject to Unavoidable Delays restore, repair, replace, and rebuild that portion of the Property not so taken to a complete architectural unit or units and as nearly as possible to the value and condition thereof immediately prior to such taking, without abatement, deduction, or set-off of any Interim Rent, Basic Rent, or Additional Rent or any other amount required to be paid by the Lessee hereunder whatsoever.

Section 15.4. If all or any part of the Property shall be taken in any such proceeding for governmental occupancy for a limited period, this Lease shall not terminate and the Lessee shall be entitled to receive the entire amount of any award made for such taking, whether paid by way of damages, rent, or otherwise, except as hereinafter set forth. In the event of such a taking for a period which extends beyond the date specifically fixed for the expiration of the term hereof, the Lessee shall be entitled to receive that portion of any award made for such taking allocable to the period of time from the date of such taking to the date specifically fixed for the expiration of the term hereof and the Lessor shall be entitled to receive the balance of such award, unless the Property is acquired by the Lessee pursuant to the next sentence hereof. If the taking for governmental occupancy shall be for a term of 1 year or more, the Lessee may offer to purchase such Property (and the Lessor's interest in any award arising out of such proceeding) at the same price, in the same manner, and subject to the same terms and conditions as are set forth in Section 15.2 in the case of a total taking.

## ARTICLE XVI

### Application of Insurance Proceeds and Condemnation Awards

Section 16.1. Unless an Event of Default shall have occurred and be continuing, any proceeds received as payment under an insurance policy for any damage or destruction and any award received by reason of a proceeding shall, except as otherwise provided in Section 14.2, 15.2, or 15.4, be held by the Trustee or, if there be no Trustee, by the Lessor (the "Depository"), and paid to the Lessee, upon request, to reimburse it for expenditures made in repairing, restoring, replacing, or rebuilding the Improvements so damaged, destroyed, or taken, payment thereof to be made as the work progresses against receipt by the Depository of proof satisfactory to it that (a) the work, to the extent performed, has been satisfactorilly accomplished; (b) the amount requested has either been paid by the Lessee or is justly due to persons who have rendered services or furnished materials in connection with the work; (c) no mechanic's, materialmen's, or similar statutory or other liens or charges have been filed against the Property; and (d) there is no outstanding indebtedness in connection with such work other than such as will be discharged in full from the amounts requested. The Depository shall not be required to apply the insurance proceeds or condemnation award as aforesaid unless it determines that the amount of the proceeds or award remaining after payment of the amount requested will be sufficient to pay in full for the completion of the repairs, restoration, replacement, or rebuilding.

Section 16.2. Upon receipt by the Depository of a certificate signed by the Lessee certifying to the completion of the repairs, restoration, replacement, or rebuilding of the Property so damaged, destroyed, or taken and the payment of the cost thereof in full, the balance of any proceeds of such insurance or any awards not required to be disbursed pursuant to Section 16.1 shall be disbursed to the Lessee.

Section 16.3. If an Event of Default shall have occurred and be continuing prior to the time for receipt of any such proceeds or awards by the Lessee pursuant to this Article, the same shall be retained by the Depository.

## ARTICLE XVII

### Default Provisions—Conditional Limitations

Section 17.1. If any one of the following events (an ''Event of Default'') shall have occurred and be continuing:

(a)   default shall be made in the payment of Interim Rent or Basic Rent when due and such default shall continue for a period of 5 days;

(b)   default shall be made in the payment of any item of Additional Rent and such default shall continue for a period of 25 days after notice thereof shall have been given to the Lessee by the Lessor;

(c)   default shall be made in the performance or observance of any other covenant or agreement of the Lessee contained herein, and such default shall continue for a period of 30 days after notice thereof shall have been given to the Lessee by the Lessor;

(d)   any representation or warranty made by the Lessee in this Lease or in any notice, certificate, report, or other information furnished in writing to the Trustee or any Registered Owner (as defined in the Indenture) of the Lessor's 11 ½ percent Secured Notes due June 1, 2010, shall be false in any material respect on the date as of which made;

(e)   the Lessee shall (1) apply for or consent to the appointment of a receiver, trustee, or liquidator of itself or of all or a substantial part of its assets, (2) be unable, or admit in writing its inability, to pay its debts as they mature, (3) make a general assignment for the benefit of creditors, (4) be adjudicated a bankrupt or insolvent, or (5) file a voluntary petition in bankruptcy or a petition or an answer seeking reorganization or an arrangement with creditors or to take advantage of any insolvency law or an answer admitting the material allegations of a petition filed against it in any bankruptcy, reorganization, or insolvency proceeding, or corporate action shall be taken by it for the purpose of effecting any of the foregoing; or

(f)   an order, judgment or decree shall be entered, without the application, approval, or consent of the Lessee, by any court of competent jurisdiction, approving a petition seeking reorganization of the Lessee, or of all or a substantial part of its assets, and such order, judgment, or decree shall continue unstayed and in effect for any period of 60 consecutive days;

the Lessor may give to the Lessee a notice of intention to end the term of this Lease at the expiration of 10 days after the date of service of such notice and at the expiration of said 10 days this Lease and all right, title, and interest of the Lessee hereunder shall terminate, unless before the expiration of said 10 days (i) all arrears in Interim Rent, Basic Rent, Additional Rent, and all other sums required to be paid by the Lessee hereunder shall have been paid in full and (ii) all other Events of Default at the time existing shall have been fully remedied. Notwithstanding such termination, the Lessee shall remain liable as hereinafter provided.

Section 17.2. Upon the termination of the term of this Lease by reason of the occurrence of any Event of Default or in the event of the termination of this Lease by summary dispossess proceedings or under any provision of law now or at any time hereafter in force, by reason of or based upon or arising out of the occurrence of an Event of Default, or upon the Lessor's recovery of possession of the Property in the manner or in any of the circumstances herein aforementioned, or in any other manner of circumstances whatsoever, whether with or without legal proceedings, by reason of or based upon or arising out of the occurrence of an Event of Default, the Lessor may, at any time, and from time to time, relet the Property or any part thereof, and receive and collect the rents therefor, apply the same first to the payment of such expenses as the Lessor may have incurred in recovering possession of the Property, including legal expenses and attorneys' fees, and for putting the same in good order or condition or preparing or altering the same for re-rental, and expenses, commissions, and charges paid, assumed or incurred by the Lessor in and about the reletting thereof, and then to the fulfillment of the covenants of the Lessee hereunder. Any such reletting herein provided for may be for the remainder of the term of this Lease or for a longer or shorter period. In any such case and whether or not the Property or any part thereof be relet, the Lessee shall pay to the Lessor all Interim Rent, Basic Rent, Additional Rent, and other sums required to be paid by the Lessee hereunder up to the time of such termination of this Lease, or of such recovery of possession of the Property by the Lessor, as the case may be. Thereafter the Lessee shall, if required by the Lessor, pay to the Lessor until the end of the term of this Lease (notwithstanding such earlier termination or recovery of possession) the equivalent of the amount of all Interim Rent, Basic Rent, Additional

Rent, and other sums required to be paid by the Lessee hereunder, less the net avails of reletting, if any, and the same shall be due and payable by the Lessee to the Lessor on the several rent days above specified, that is to say, upon each of such rent days the Lessee shall pay to the Lessor the amount of the deficiency then existing. In any of the circumstances herein above mentioned in which the Lessor shall have the right to hold the Lessee liable upon the several rent days herein specified to pay to the Lessor the equivalent of the amount of all Interim Rent, Basic Rent, Additional Rent, and other sums required to be paid by the Lessee hereunder less the net avails of reletting, if any, the Lessor shall have the election in place and in stead of holding the Lessee so liable forthwith to recover against the Lessee, as damages for loss of the bargain and not as a penalty, an aggregate sum which, at the time of such termination of this Lease, or of such recovery of possession of the Property by the Lessor, as the case may be, represents the then present worth of the excess, if any, of the aggregate of all Interim Rent, Basic Rent, Additional Rent, and other sums required to be paid by the Lessee hereunder that would have accrued for the balance of the term of this Lease over the aggregate rental value of the Property for the balance of such term, but in no event less than the then outstanding principal of, premium, if any, and accrued interest on, the Notes.

Section 17.3. The Lessee hereby expressly waives the service of notice of intention to reenter provided for in any statute now or hereafter in force, or to institute legal proceedings to that end, and also waives any and all right of redemption provided for in any statute now or hereafter in force in case the Lessee shall be dispossessed by a judgment or by warrant of any court or judge. The Lesssee also waives and will waive any and all right to a trial by a jury provided for in any statute now or hereafter in force in the event that summary proceedings or any other action or proceeding shall be instituted by the Lessor. The terms "enter," "reenter," "entry" or "reentry," as used in this Lease, are not restricted to their technical legal meeting.


## ARTICLE XVIII

### Indemnity

Section 18.1. The Lessee shall indemnify and save the Lessor harmless against and from any and all liability, fines, suits, claims, demands, expenses, and actions of any kind or nature arising by reason of injury to person or property occurring on or about the Property. The Lessee shall maintain workmen's compensation insurance, or cause the same to be maintained, at all times when any Alterations to the Property are in progress. The Lessee shall defend the Lessor against any of the foregoing by counsel selected by the Lessee. The Lessor shall promptly notify the Lessee of any of the foregoing known to the Lessor, but the failure of the Lessor to do so shall not impair the obligations of the Lessee hereunder.

## ARTICLE XIX

### Economic Abandonment of the Property

Section 19.1. If, at any time on or after June 1, 1990 and before the expiration or earlier termination of this Lease, the Lessee certifies in writing to the Lessor that it is no longer feasible to operate the Property in the conduct of the Lessee's business and that, promptly after its purchase thereof, the Lessee intends to dispose of the Property to a person not affiliated with the Lessee or abandon the Property, the Lessee, provided no Event of Default shall have occurred and be continuing, may offer to purchase the Property in accordance with the provisions of Article XXI at the purchase price calculated in Schedule II hereto, together with a premium equal to 5 percent of the Capitalized Cost of the Property (as defined in Schedule II).

## ARTICLE XX

### Offer to Purchase Property at End of Basic Term

Section 20.1. The Lessee shall, on not less than 12 months' notice to the Lessor, offer to purchase the Property on the expiration date of the Basic Term in accordance with the provisions of Article XXI at a price equal to the purchase price calculated in Schedule II hereto.

## ARTICLE XXI

### Procedure on Purchase of the Property

Section 21.1. If the Lessee is required or elects to offer to purchase the Property pursuant to Sections 11.2, 14.2, 15.2, 15.4, 19.1, or 20.1, the Lessee, in such offer, shall specify a date and place for such purchase, which date shall be not less than 30 days nor more than 45 days after the date of the making of such offer.

Section 21.2. If the Lessor accepts such offer, the Lessee's purchase of the Property shall be closed on the date and at the place specified in the offer, and the Lessor shall deliver or cause to be delivered to the Lessee on such date a deed or other instrument or instruments conveying the Lessor's interest in the Property to the Lessee or its designee and the Lessee shall make payment of the purchase price therefor by delivering to the Lessor a certified or official bank check in the required amount. Such instrument of conveyance shall contain a covenant by the Lessor that the Property was not sold or otherwise conveyed by the Lessor and is free and clear of any lien, mortgage, or encumbrance created by the affirmative act of the Lessor, other than Permitted Encumbrances and any interest created by the Lessor or the Trustee upon the request of the Lessee, the Lessor otherwise being obligated to give only such right, title, and interest as it is able to convey, but the truth or validity of such covenant shall not be a condition to the Lessee's obligation to pay such purchase price in the event that the Lessee is required to purchase the Lessor's interest in the Property. If it should become necessary for the Trustee or any other party to institute any foreclosure or other judicial proceeding in order to be able to convey the Lessor's interest in the Property or any part thereof, the time within which delivery of the deed or other instrument of conveyance may be made shall be extended to the extent necessary to permit the Trustee or such other party to institute and conclude any such legal proceeding and the Lessee shall remain liable on this Lease for the period of such extension. Upon the purchase of the Property, the term of this Lease and all right, title, and interest of the Lessee hereunder shall terminate, except that the Lessee shall remain liable for all obligations accrued hereunder prior to such termination.

Section 21.3. If the Lessor rejects an offer to purchase the Property or fails to accept the same, this Lease, unless renewed in accordance with Section 2.3, shall terminate on the date specified in such offer for the purchase of the Property. Notwithstanding anything to the contrary herein contained, the Lessor shall not reject such offer or fail to accept the same without the consent of the Registered Owners (as defined in the Indenture) of at least a majority in principal amount of the Lessor's 11 ½ percent Secured Notes due June 1, 2010 issued under the secured by the Indenture. The failure of said Registered Owners to consent to any such rejection or failure to accept shall be deemed to constitute an acceptance by the Lessor of the Lessee's offer to purchase the Property.

Section 21.4. Upon any purchase made pursuant to the provisions of this Article, the Lessee shall pay to the Lessor all costs and expenses (including, without limitations, all taxes, including Federal and State documentary stamp taxes, and all attorneys' fees and expenses) of the Lessor, incurred in conjunction with such purchase.

## ARTICLE XXII

### Assignment and Subletting

Section 22.1. The interest of the Lessee in this Lease may be assigned or transferred in whole but not in part, by the Lessee or by any assignee of the Lessee, and all or any part of the Property may be sublet, provided, however, that the assignee or transferee shall execute and deliver to the Lessor and the Trustee an instrument, satisfactory to the Lessor and the Trustee, assuming all the obligations of the Lessee hereunder. No assignment, transfer, or sublease, and no such instrument of assumption, shall affect or reduce any of the obligations of the Lessee hereunder, but this Lease and all obligations of the Lessee hereunder shall continue in full force and effect as the obligations of a principal and not as the obligations of a guarantor or surety. No extension of time for the payment of any amount hereunder, no waiver of any term of this Lease or of any Event of Default hereunder or other indulgence of any nature whatsoever estended in any manner by the Lessor to any such assignee, transferee, or sublessee, with or without notice to or assent from the Lessee, shall relieve the Lessee of any of its obligations under this Lease.

## ARTICLE XXIII

### Cumulative Remedies—No Waiver

Section 23.1. The specific remedies to which the Lessor may resort under the terms of this Lease are cumulative and are not intended to be exclusive of any other remedies or means of redress to which it may be lawfully entitled in case of any Event of Default. The failure of the Lessor to insist in any one or more cases upon the strict performance of any of the convenants of this Lease, or to exercise any option herein contained, shall not be construed as a waiver or relinquishment for the future of such covenant or option. A receipt by the Lessor of rent with knowledge of the occurrence of an Event of Default shall not be deemed a waiver thereof, and no waiver, change, modification, or discharge by either party hereto of any provision in this Lease shall be deemed to have been made or shall be effective unless expressed in writing and signed by the party against whom such waiver, change, modification, or discharge is sought. In addition to the other remedies in this Lease provided, the Lessor shall be entitled to the restraint by injunction of the violation, or attempted or threatened violation, of any of the covenants, conditions, or provisions of this Lease or to a decree compelling specific performance of any of such covenants, conditions, or provisions.

## ARTICLE XXIV

### Quiet Enjoyment

Section 24.1. The Lessee, upon paying the Interim Rent, Basic Rent, Additional Rent, and all other sums required to be paid by the Lessee hereunder and observing and keeping the covenants, agreements, and conditions of this Lease on its part to be kept, shall and may peaceably and quietly hold, occupy, and enjoy the Property during the term of this Lease without hindrance of molestation by or from anyone claiming by, through, or under the Lessor.

## ARTICLE XXV

### Notices

Section 25.1. All notices, demands, consents, requests, and other communications hereunder which may or are required to be given by any pary to the others shall be in writing and shall be deemed to have been properly given when sent by United States registered or certified mail, postage prepaid, addressed (a) if to the parties hereto, at their respective addresses set forth above, or at such other address as any party may from time to time designate in a notice to the others, (b) if to the Trustee, at its address set forth in the Indenture, or at such other address as the Trustee may from time to time designate in a notice to the Lessee, and (c) if to the Registered Owners, c/o the Trustee, at its address set forth in the Indenture, or at such other address as the Trustee may from time to time designate in a notice to the Lessee.

## ARTICLE XXVI

### Invalidity of Particular Provisions

Section 26.1. If any term or provision of this Lease or the application thereof to any person or circumstance shall, to any extent, be invalid or unenforceable, the remainder of this Lease, or the application of such term or provision to persons or circumstances other than those as to which it is held invalid or unenforceable, shall not be affected thereby, and each term and provision of this Lease shall be valid and enforceable to the fullest extent permitted by law.

# ARTICLE XXVII

## Financial Statements, Estoppel Certificates

Section 27.1. The Lessee shall deliver to the Lessor, the Trustee, and the Registered Owners from time to time during the term of this Lease:

(a) as soon as practicable in any event within 60 days after the end of each of the first three quarterly fiscal periods in each fiscal year of the Lessee, a consolidated and consolidating statement of income of the Lessee for the period from the beginning of the current fiscal year to the end of such quarterly period, and a consolidated and consolidating balance sheet of the Lessee as at the end of such quarterly period, all in reasonable detail and certified by an authorized financial officer of the Lessee, subject to changes resulting from year-end and audit adjustments;

(b) as soon as practicable and in any event within 120 days after the end of each such fiscal year, consolidated and consolidating statements of income, retained earnings, and changes in financial position of the Lessee for such year, and a consolidated and consolidating balance sheet of the Lessee as at the end of such year, all in reasonable detail and, in the case of consolidated financial statements, certified to the Lessee by an independent public accountant of recognized standing selected by the Lessee and satisfactory to the Lessor, the Trustee, and the Registered Owners;

(c) as soon as practicable and in any event within 120 days after the end of each such fiscal year, a certificate of the insurer under the insurance policies maintained by the Lessee pursuant to Article V or of an independent insurance underwriter of recognized standing to the effect that such insurance complies with all of the requirements of Article V;

(d) within 30 days after June 1 in each year beginning with the year 1981, an opinion of counsel for the Lessee, dated as of such opinion date, either stating that, in the opinion of such counsel, such action has been taken with respect to the filing, registration, recording, re-filing, re-registration, and re-recording of the Indenture, this Lease, the Assignment, and/or any financing statement or similar instrument, and of each supplemental indenture or other instrument of further assurance or other document relating to any thereof, as is necessary to maintain and preserve the validity of the Indenture, this Lease and the Assignment, or the lien of the Indenture, and setting forth the particulars of such action, or stating that, in the opinion of such counsel, no such action is necessary to maintain and preserve such lien and validity;

(e) as soon as practicable, copies of (i) all periodic reports on Forms 10-Q and 10-K under the Securities Exchange Act of 1934 and prospectuses filed pursuant to Rule 424(b) under the Securities Act of 1933, and (ii) all such financial statements, proxy statements, and reports as the Lessee shall send to its stockholders; and

(f)   such other information relating to the performance of the provisions of the Indenture, this Lease, and the Assignment, and to the affairs of the Lessee and its subsidiaries as the Lessor, the Trustee, or the Registered Owners may from time to time reasonably request including, without limitation, any information, to the extent the Lessee possesses such information or can acquire it without unreasonable effort or expense, necessary to verify the accuracy of any of the representations and warranties made by the Lessee in any instrument delivered to the Lessor, the Trustee, or the Registered Owners in connection with the transactions contemplated by the Indenture, this Lease, and the Assignment.

Section 27.2. The Lessee shall, upon not less than 20 days' prior notice to the Lessee by the Lessor, execute, acknowledge, and deliver to the Lessor a certificate stating (a) that the Lessee knows of no condition or event which constitutes an Event of Default or which, with notice or lapse of time or both, would constitute an Event of Default, or, if any such condition or event exists, specifying the nature and period of existence thereof and what action the Lessee is taking or proposes to take with respect thereto; (b) that this Lease is unmodified and in full force and effect (or, if modified, stating the modifications and certifying that as so modified, This Lease is in full force and effect); and (c) the dates to which the Basic Rent has been paid.

## ARTICLE XXVIII

### Memorandum of the Lease

Section 28.1. The Lessor and the Lessee shall, promptly upon the request of either, enter into a short form memorandum of this Lease, in substantially the form of Schedule III hereto and otherwise suitable for record under the laws of the State in which the Property is located, in which reference to this Lease shall be made.

## ARTICLE XXIX

### Covenants to Bind and Benefit Respective Parties

Section 29.1. The convenants and agreements herein contained shall bind and inure to the benefit of the Lessor and the Lessee, and their respective successors and assigns.

Section 29.2. The term "Lessor" as used in this Lease means only the owner or the mortgagee or trustee in possession of the Property (or the lessee of a ground or underlying lease of the Property or of the Improvements) from time to time, so that in the event of any sale or transfer of the Property or of said ground or underlying lease, or in the event of a lease of the Property or of the Improvements, the Lessor shall be and hereby is released from its obligations as lessor hereunder, and with the purchaser, transferee, or lessee, as the case may be, without any further agreement between the parties hereto or their successors in interest, shall be deemed to have assumed all of the obligations of the Lessor hereunder.

## ARTICLE XXX

### Expenses

Section 30.1. The Lessee shall pay (a) the organizational expenses of the Lessor, (b) all expenses required by the Indenture to be paid by the Lessor in connection with the execution and delivery of the Indenture, this Lease, and the Assigment and related documents, and the consummation of the transactions contemplated thereby, including, without limitation, commitment fees, payment of title insurance premiums, printing or duplicating expenses, recording fees and taxes, the fees and expenses of counsel, and reasonable compensation to the Trustee, and (c) all operating and other expenses incurred by the Lessor in connection with or related to the Lessor's business of leasing the Property to the Lessee and issuing and servicing the Notes including, without limitation, the out-of-pocket expenses of the Lessor in connection with any purchase of the Property, but excluding (i) any income, franchise, and other taxes which may be incurred by the Lessor during the term of this Lease, (ii) the principal of, premium, if any, and interest on the Notes, and (iii) any net income taxes of the Lessor based upon the receipt by the Lessor of any excess of the Basic Rent over Note Payments (as defined in the Indenture).

## ARTICLE XXXI

### No Offsets

Section 31.1. The Lessee represents and warrants that it has no offsets or defenses to the enforcement of any remedies the Lessor may have by operation of law or in the event of default by the Lessee in the performance or observance of any of the terms, convenants, or conditions of this Lease.

## ARTICLE XXXII

### Investment Credit

Section 32.1. The Lessee shall be entitled to claim and receive the investment credit allowed by §38 of the Internal Revenue Code of 1954, as amended, or under the corresponding section of any United States income tax law at any time in effect during the term of this Lease.

IN WITNESS WHEREOF, the parties hereto have caused this Lease to be duly executed as of the day and year first above written.

## SCHEDULE II

### Purchase Prices of the Property

The Capitalized Cost of the Property as of any date is $5,830,000.

If purchased pursuant to Section 11.2, 14.2, 15.2, 15.4, 19.1, or 20.1 of this Lease, the purchase price of the Property shall be determined by multiplying the Capitalized Cost of the Property by the percentage set forth below.

| Purchased During Quarter-Annual Period Immediately Following the Following Dates (a "Basic Rent Payment Date"): | Purchase Price* Expressed as a Percentage of the Capitalized Cost of the Property |
|---|---|
| June 1, 1980† | 97.323 |
| September 1, 1980 | 97.201 |
| December 1, 1980 | 97.075 |
| March 1, 1981 | 96.946 |
| June 1, 1981 | 96.813 |
| September 1, 1981 | 96.677 |
| December 1, 1981 | 96.537 |
| March 1, 1982 | 96.394 |
| June 1, 1982 | 96.247 |
| September 1, 1982 | 96.096 |
| December 1, 1982 | 95.941 |
| March 1, 1983 | 95.783 |
| June 1, 1983 | 95.619 |
| September 1, 1983 | 95.452 |

| Purchased During Quarter-Annual Period Immediately Following the Following Dates (a "Basic Rent Payment Date"): | Purchase Price* Expressed as a Percentage of the Capitalized Cost of the Property |
|---|---|
| December 1, 1983 | 95.280 |
| March 1, 1984 | 95.104 |
| June 1, 1984 | 94.923 |
| September 1, 1984 | 94.738 |
| December 1, 1984 | 94.547 |
| March 1, 1985 | 94.352 |
| June 1, 1985 | 94.151 |
| September 1, 1985 | 93.945 |
| December 1, 1985 | 93.734 |
| March 1, 1986 | 93.517 |
| June 1, 1986 | 93.294 |
| September 1, 1986 | 93.066 |
| December 1, 1986 | 92.832 |
| March 1, 1987 | 92.591 |
| June 1, 1987 | 92.344 |
| September 1, 1987 | 92.091 |
| December 1, 1987 | 91.831 |
| March 1, 1988 | 91.564 |
| June 1, 1988 | 91.290 |
| September 1, 1988 | 91.009 |
| December 1, 1988 | 90.721 |
| March 1, 1989 | 90.425 |
| June 1, 1989 | 90.121 |
| September 1, 1989 | 89.810 |
| December 1, 1989 | 89.490 |
| March 1, 1990 | 89.162 |
| June 1, 1990 | 88.825 |
| September 1, 1990 | 88.479 |
| December 1, 1990 | 88.124 |
| March 1, 1991 | 87.760 |
| June 1, 1991 | 87.387 |
| September 1, 1991 | 87.003 |
| December 1, 1991 | 86.610 |
| March 1, 1992 | 86.206 |

| Purchased During Quarter-Annual Period Immediately Following the Following Dates (a "Basic Rent Payment Date"): | Purchase Price* Expressed as a Percentage of the Capitalized Cost of the Property |
|---|---|
| June 1, 1992 | 85.791 |
| September 1, 1992 | 85.366 |
| December 1, 1992 | 84.929 |
| March 1, 1993 | 84.482 |
| June 1, 1993 | 84.022 |
| September 1, 1993 | 83.550 |
| December 1, 1993 | 83.066 |
| March 1, 1994 | 82.569 |
| June 1, 1994 | 82.059 |
| September 1, 1994 | 81.536 |
| December 1, 1994 | 80.999 |
| March 1, 1995 | 80.448 |
| June 1, 1995 | 79.882 |
| September 1, 1995 | 79.301 |
| December 1, 1995 | 78.706 |
| March 1, 1996 | 78.094 |
| June 1, 1996 | 77.467 |
| September 1, 1996 | 76.823 |
| December 1, 1996 | 76.162 |
| March 1, 1997 | 75.484 |
| June 1, 1997 | 74.788 |
| September 1, 1997 | 74.074 |
| December 1, 1997 | 73.341 |
| March 1, 1998 | 72.589 |
| June 1, 1998 | 71.817 |
| September 1, 1998 | 71.025 |
| December 1, 1998 | 70.212 |
| March 1, 1999 | 69.378 |
| June 1, 1999 | 68.522 |
| September 1, 1999 | 67.643 |
| December 1, 1999 | 66.741 |
| March 1, 2000 | 65.816 |
| June 1, 2000 | 64.866 |
| September 1, 2000 | 63.892 |

| Purchased During Quarter-Annual Period Immediately Following the Following Dates (a "Basic Rent Payment Date"): | Purchase Price* Expressed as a Percentage of the Capitalized Cost of the Property |
|---|---|
| December 1, 2000 | 62.892 |
| March 1, 2001 | 61.865 |
| June 1, 2001 | 60.812 |
| September 1, 2001 | 59.731 |
| December 1, 2001 | 58.621 |
| March 1, 2002 | 57.483 |
| June 1, 2002 | 56.314 |
| September 1, 2002 | 55.115 |
| December 1, 2002 | 53.885 |
| March 1, 2003 | 52.622 |
| June 1, 2003 | 51.326 |
| September 1, 2003 | 49.996 |
| December 1, 2003 | 48.631 |
| March 1, 2004 | 47.230 |
| June 1, 2004 | 45.792 |
| September 1, 2004 | 44.317 |
| December 1, 2004 | 42.803 |
| March 1, 2005 | 41.249 |
| June 1, 2005 | 39.654 |
| September 1, 2005 | 38.018 |
| December 1, 2005 | 36.339 |
| March 1, 2006 | 34.615 |
| June 1, 2006 | 32.846 |
| September 1, 2006 | 31.031 |
| December 1, 2006 | 29.169 |
| March 1, 2007 | 27.257 |
| June 1, 2007 | 25.295 |
| September 1, 2007 | 23.282 |
| December 1, 2007 | 21.215 |
| March 1, 2008 | 19.095 |
| June 1, 2008 | 16.919 |
| September 1, 2008 | 14.686 |
| December 1, 2008 | 12.394 |
| March 1, 2009 | 10.042 |

| Purchased During Quarter-Annual Period Immediately Following the Following Dates (a "Basic Rent Payment Date"): | Purchase Price* Expressed as a Percentage of the Capitalized Cost of the Property |
|---|---|
| June 1, 2009 | 7.628 |
| September 1, 2009 | 5.151 |
| December 1, 2009 | 2.609 |
| March 1, 2010 | 0.000 |

*Plus interest thereon from the immediately preceding Basic Rent Payment Date to the date fixed for purchase at the rate of 10½ percent per annum (on a 30 day month and 360 day year basis), together with an amount equal to the applicable prepayment premium, if any, on the Notes.

†The purchase price during the period prior to June 1, 1980 shall be equal to 100 percent of the Capitalized Cost of the Property plus the interest thereon from the date of commencement of the Interim Term or the first day of the month in which the purchase occurs, whichever is later, to the date fixed for purchase at the rate of 10½ percent per annum (computed as shown in the schedule).

# Chapter 5

# ECONOMICS OF LEASE FINANCING

This chapter will cover the economics of leasing, including, among other things, lease versus buy analysis.

Most lease versus buy analyses result in the conclusion that buying is economically preferable to leasing. In this chapter, we will attempt to show why this conclusion may not be universally true and why in many cases leasing will be economically preferable to buying.

Before we embark on the more complicated lease versus buy analyses, we need to review the fundamentals of present value calculations and discounting. The more advanced reader may skip this section.

## THE TIME VALUE OF MONEY

Economists have long recognized that money has a time value, which is usually referred to as interest. To be more specific, it is generally accepted that if you are willing to forego the immediate use of your money and are willing to let others use it, then you are entitled to receive a payment called interest.

Accountants have not always explicitly recognized the interest aspect of financial measurements. However, with the issuance of Accounting Principles Board Opinion No. 21, in 1971, it became apparent that the concept of the time value of money would eventually permeate most areas of accounting, including leasing.

The essence of calculations involving the time value of money concept consists in two basic and simple mathematical formulas: (1) the compound interest formula and (2) the ordinary annuity formula.

### Compound Interest Formula

If  $P$ = principal
 $i$ = interest rate

$n$ = number of compounding periods
$A$ = amount

then

amount at time $0 = A_0 = P$

and

amount at time $1 = A_1 = P + Pi = P(1 + i)$

and

amount at time $2 = A_2 = A_1 + A_1 i$
$$= P(1 + i) + P(1 + i) = P(1 + i)(1 + i)$$
$$= P(1 + i)^2$$

Therefore

amount at time $n = A_n = P(1 + i)^n$

With this formula we can answer a question such as the following: If you deposit $1000 in a bank account bearing interest at 6 percent compounded annually, how much will accumulate in 10 years?

*Answer*   $1790.85

*Solution*   $A_{10} = (1000)(1+0.06)^{10} = 1000(1.79085)$

A calculator or present value tables may be used to make this calculation.
    Often we would like to know how much money we need to set aside in order to accumulate a known amount at the end of a certain period of time. This is simply the inverse of the preceding example. For instance, if we want to answer a question such as the following: If $10,000 is desired in 20 years, how much do you need to deposit today if the account bears interest at 6 percent compounded annually?

*Answer*   $3118.00

*Solution*          $A_{20} = 10,000 = P(1+0.06)^{20}$

$$P = \frac{10,000}{(1 + 0.06)^{20}} = 10,000 \frac{1}{(1 + 0.06)^{20}}$$

$$= 10,000(0.31180) = \$3118.00$$

Again, a calculator or time value of money tables may be used to make this calculation.

We can solve more complicated problems in a similar manner. For example, let us say you have the right to receive rents as follows:

|  |  |
|---|---|
| December 31, 1980 | $4000 |
| December 31, 1981 | 5000 |
| December 31, 1982 | 6000 |

A bank is willing to buy your right to receive these rents, but at a discount of 8 percent per year compounded annually. How much would the bank pay you or January 1, 1980?

*Answer* $12,753.38

*Solution*

$$P = \frac{A_1}{(1 + i)^1} + \frac{A_2}{(1 + i)^2} + \frac{A_3}{(1 + i)^3}$$

$P$ is the amount the bank will pay. $A_1$, $A_2$, $A_3$ are the rents.

$$P = 4000 \left(\frac{1}{(1 + 0.08)^1}\right) + 5000 \left(\frac{1}{(1 + 0.08)^2}\right) + 6000 \left(\frac{1}{(1 + 0.08)^3}\right)$$

$$P = 4000(0.92593) + 5000(0.85734) + 6000(0.79383)$$

$$P = \$12,753.38$$

## Ordinary Annuity Formula

In the previous example, if all the rents had been equal at $4000, then the stream of rents would be defined as an ordinary annuity.

Often we want to know the future value or the present value of an ordinary annuity. For example, a noncancelable lease of 10 years is equivalent to a 10 year annuity from the lessor's perspective.

The formula for the future value of an ordinary annuity of $1 per period is found as follows:

$$\text{future value} = A = 1 + (1 + i) + (1 + i)^2 + \ldots + (1 + i)^n$$

Perhaps you recognize this as the sum of a geometric progression where (1

+ $i$) is the common element. The fact that it is a geometric progression allows us to simplify the formula as follows:

$$\text{future value} = A = \frac{(1 + i)^n - 1}{i} \cdot R$$

where $R$ is the periodic rent.

We can now answer questions such as if you put $150 per year in a savings account bearing interest at 6 percent compounded annually, how much will it grow to in 5 years?

*Answer*    *$845.46*

*Solution*

$$A = \frac{(1 + 0.06)^5 - 1}{0.06}(150) = 5.63709\,(150) = 845.46$$

We also would like to know the present value of ordinary annuities, because the amount of a capitalized lease is really the present value of an annuity. A formula has been derived to find this present value.

present value of ordinary annuity

$$= PV_A = \frac{(1 + i)^n - 1}{i} \cdot \frac{1}{(1 + i)^n} \cdot R$$

$$PV_A = \frac{1 - \dfrac{1}{(1 + i)^n}}{i} \cdot R$$

where R is the annual rent.

In the example where we assumed that you have rents receivable in the future as follows:

|                      |        |
|----------------------|--------|
| December 31, 1980    | $4000  |
| December 31, 1981    | 4000   |
| December 31, 1982    | 4000   |

and a bank is willing to buy your right to receive these rents, but at an 8 percent discount compounded annually. How much would the bank be willing to pay at January 1, 1980?

*Answer*    $10,692.05

*Solution*

$$P = 4000 \cdot \frac{1 - \dfrac{1}{(1 + 0.08)^3}}{0.08}$$

$$P = 4000(2.57710)$$

$$P = 10,692.05$$

## TIME VALUE OF MONEY IN LEASE VERSUS BUY ANALYSIS

In Chapter 1, we briefly touched on lease versus buy analysis (see Exhibit 1.1). In Exhibit 1.1 we assumed that a company will acquire a piece of equipment costing $100,000. The company has a choice of acquiring the equipment by borrowing the $100,000 at 10 percent interest, to be repaid in ten equal installments of $16,270 per year, or by leasing the machine for $16,270 per year. There is an investment tax credit of 10 percent multiplied by the cost of the machine ($100,000 × 10 percent = $10,000), which the firm will get whether it buys or leases (i.e., the investment tax credit will be passed through to the lessee).

In Exhibit 1.1 we compared the costs of ownership with the costs of leasing. (Exhibit 1.1 is duplicated here as Exhibit 5.1). The costs of ownership are found as follows:

1 Debt service payments equal to principal reduction and interest expense on the $100,000 loan ($16,270 per year).

2 Less the tax benefits* of ownership, arising from:

   (a) Depreciation expense deductions on the cost of the equipment ($100,000 per year straight-line depreciation times 46 percent tax rate) (see Exhibit 5.1, line 5).

   (b) Interest expense deductions (interest expense times the 46 percent tax rate) (Exhibit 5.1, line 3).

   (c) The investment tax credit (Exhibit 5.1, line 6).

The net cost or benefit of ownership is shown in Exhibit 5.1, line 7.

In comparison, the cost of leasing is equal to the rent expense ($16,270 per year) less the tax benefit arising from rent expense deductions ($16,270 × 46

---

*The existence of a tax benefit is predicated on the business enterprises having taxable income from other sources against which tax deductions for depreciation, interest, and rent expenses may be taken.

*Exhibit 5.1* Comparison of Cost of Leasing with Ownership

| | | 1 | 2 | 3 | 4 | 5 | 6 | 7 | 8 | 9 | 10 | Total |
|---|---|---|---|---|---|---|---|---|---|---|---|---|
| **Ownership** | | | | | | | | | | | | |
| (1) | Debt service | $16,270 | $16,270 | $16,270 | $16,270 | $16,270 | $16,270 | $16,270 | $16,270 | $16,270 | $16,270 | $162,700 |
| (2) | Interest portion | 10,000 | 9,370 | 8,680 | 7,920 | 7,090 | 6,170 | 5,160 | 4,050 | 2,800 | 1,460 | 62,700 |
| (3) | Tax benefits (46 percent) | 4,600 | 4,310 | 3,990 | 3,640 | 3,260 | 2,840 | 2,370 | 1,860 | 1,290 | 680 | 28,840 |
| (4) | Depreciation | 10,000 | 10,000 | 10,000 | 10,000 | 10,000 | 10,000 | 10,000 | 10,000 | 10,000 | 10,000 | 100,000 |
| (5) | Tax benefits (46 percent) | 4,600 | 4,600 | 4,600 | 4,600 | 4,600 | 4,600 | 4,600 | 4,600 | 4,600 | 4,600 | 46,000 |
| (6) | Investment tax credit | 10,000 | — | — | — | — | — | — | — | — | — | 10,000 |
| (7) | Net (cost) benefit of ownership (3) + (5) + (6) − (1) | 2,930 | (7,360) | (7,680) | (8,030) | (8,410) | (8,830) | (9,300) | (9,810) | (10,380) | (10,930) | $(77,860) |
| **Leasing** | | | | | | | | | | | | |
| (8) | Rent | $16,270 | $16,270 | $16,270 | $16,270 | $16,270 | $16,270 | $16,270 | $16,270 | $16,270 | $16,270 | $162,700 |
| (9) | Tax benefits (46 percent) | 7,480 | 7,480 | 7,480 | 7,480 | 7,480 | 7,490 | 7,490 | 7,490 | 7,490 | 7,490 | 74,840 |
| (10) | Investment tax credit | 10,000 | — | — | — | — | — | — | — | — | — | 10,000 |
| (11) | Net (cost) benefit of leasing | 1,210 | (8,790) | (8,790) | (8,790) | (8,790) | (8,780) | (8,780) | (8,780) | (8,780) | (8,780) | (77,860) |
| (12) | Net benefit (cost) of ownership (7) − (11) | $ 1,710 | $ 1,430 | $ 1,110 | $ 760 | $ 380 | $ (50) | $ (520) | $ (1,030) | $ (1,600) | $ (2,190) | $ 0 |
| (13) | Present value of net benefit (cost) of ownership discounted @ 10 percent | $1,554.50 | $1,181.80 | $834.00 | $519.10 | $236.00 | $(28.20) | $(266.80) | $(480.50) | $(678.60) | $(844.50) | $2,705.60 |

percent) (Exhibit 5.1, line 9). The net cost or benefit of leasing is shown in Exhibit 5.1, line 11.

The net benefit in favor of ownership or leasing is equal to the difference between the net cost or benefit of ownership and the net cost or benefit of leasing. The net benefit of ownership in the example is shown in Exhibit 5.1, line 12.

In Exhibit 1.1, line 12 was the last line in the table. The amounts shown in that line were added across to show the total net benefit of ownership, which in that example was zero.

In Exhibit 5.1, an additional line (line 13) has been added to the table to take into consideration the time value of money. Each of the numbers in line 12 has been discounted back to the beginning of the lease term in order to give the present value of each period's benefit. The present values appear in line 13.

For example, the amount in line 13, column 5 is found by multiplying line 12, column 5 ($380) by the present value of $1 to be received 5 years in the future, discounted at 10 percent (0.61391):

$$(\$380) \left( \frac{1}{(1 + 0.10)^5} \right) = (\$380)(0.61391) = \$236.00$$

The result of applying the time value of money concept to the lease versus buy analysis indicates a preference for owning in this particular example. The present value of the net benefit of ownership is $2705.60.

Some experts in finance have argued that present value analysis will always result in a conclusion that the present value net benefit of ownership exceeds the present value net benefit of leasing. The next section discusses some of the economic rationale in favor of leasing.

## THE ECONOMIC RATIONALE OF LEASING

The purpose of a business enterprise is to combine financial capital, raw materials, and labor in the proper mix and as a result create more financial capital than there was originally. It is theoretically unnecessary, as an intermediate step, to acquire tangible capital in the form of owned assets. From the business entity's perspective, the simple use of the assets should be equally satisfactory.

Ownership is, however, more prevalent than leasing in the real world. Contributing heavily to the desire to own is the tax deduction allowed by the Internal Revenue Code for depreciation of owned property, plant, or equipment. This, when combined with interest expense deductions on the necessary financing required to own, often exceeds the rent deduction allowable on leased property, plant, or equipment. In addition, the residual value of the leased property at the end of the lease term is retained with ownership but lost through leasing.

Therefore, there is a positive incentive to own unless:

1  The business does not pay income taxes.
2  The useful life of that which would be owned or leased is so short that the tax benefits of ownership are irrelevant and the residual value is immaterial.
3  Ownership is not possible.

If an entity is not a taxpayer, either permanently (e.g., an entity not taxed) or temporarily, then the tax incentive of ownership is lost. If the entity persists in owning, it may suffer real economic consequences. Therefore, a market has developed to allocate tax benefits from those who cannot take advantage of such benefits to whose who can. This is a principal purpose of leasing. Leasing allows unfettered use of property with simultaneous transfer of tax benefits to unrelated parties.

Finally, certain assets have short useful lives, and therefore the tax benefits of ownership and residual values are irrelevant in a lease versus ownership decision analysis. For example, such assets may include computers and other office equipment or vehicle fleets. In addition, economies of scale may exist in performance of maintenance on such equipment by the leasing company. It is clear that the economic reality of leases of this nature rests in the use of the assets rather than ownership. Reflection in financial statements of such assets as owned assets would appear to be contrary to economic reality.

To summarize, therefore, leasing has arisen in response to an economic need to:

1  Transfer tax benefits to those who can use them most appropriately.
2  Provide use, rather than ownership, of assets that have relatively short lives.
3  Provide access to assets when ownership is difficult or impossible.

In capsule form, lack of ability to take advantage of tax benefits, shortness of useful life, and ownership prevention are the three primary economic rationale of leasing.

In a capitalist economy, entrepreneurs will attempt to gain economic control of scarce resources (e.g., oil bearing properties, timber lands, choice suburban real estate, or uranium) and then exploit such assets until the market demand is exhausted. Leasing is a means of gaining economic control. Hence entrepreneurs may have desirable assets, and although they will not sell such assets, they will lease them. Nuclear reactor cores could not be purchased in recent periods, but could be leased. Real estate in all areas of the country cannot be purchased, but may be leased. In essence, when ownership of the asset is not a feasible option, leasing is mandated.

One may be prevented in other ways from owning property. Most municipal and state legislatures prevent purchases of certain assets by governmental authorities without elaborate approvals or even voter concurrence. This often leads governments toward leasing rather than owning.

Public utilities, in many jurisdictions, have difficulty obtaining rate increases in amounts sufficient to permit the financing of new plant and equipment. Hence ownership is in essence precluded. Alternatively, rental expense may be directly allowable as a cost of service, thus producing a positive incentive toward leasing.

Although the implicit interest rate in a lease is often higher than the rate at which a firm could borrow money, leasing may be preferred, for the reasons indicated previously. Tax considerations are a primary consideration in most leasing arrangements. When a company cannot benefit from the depreciation tax shield or the investment credit, it may obtain a lower effective interest rate by allowing a lessor to take advantage of these tax benefits. For example, if, in Exhibit 5.1, the company was not able to take advantage of the tax benefits of ownership, there would be a net benefit to leasing caused by the fact that the lessor would retain the investment tax credit and the right to depreciate the equipment and, therefore, should reduce the annual rental below the $16,270 stated in the exhibit. The amount of the reduction would be dependent on the tax position of the lessor, the length of the lease, and the credit rating of the lessee, among other factors. Clearly, the lessee is attempting to achieve the lowest cost of financing congruent with the fact that he is not in a tax paying position (thus indicating operating losses) and therefore may not be a strong credit risk.

There are other reasons for leasing. In industries where there is rapid technological innovation, the risk of obsolescence may be assumed by a lessor who is able to spread such risk among a number of lessees and over multiple assets. In addition, equipment leasing can provide flexibility that may not be available through other methods of financing. For example, lease contracts often do not have restrictive covenants or prohibitions against further debt. To the extent that a source of financing through leasing is made available to firms that are unable to secure financing from conventional sources, the leasing tends to smooth out imperfections in the capital markets.

Other advantages claimed for leasing may not be totally justified. Improving a company's financial position through off-balance sheet financing has been discredited since it depends on the lack of sophistication of the financial analyst. However, off-balance sheet financing is still given as a reason for leasing, even by leasing experts. Because of the lower initial cash outflow provided by leasing as opposed to ownership, leasing does help preserve working capital. However, the continuing cash outflow with leasing may overshadow its initial cash savings.

The advantages of leasing are more apparent in financial leases than in operating leases. A financial lease is essentially an extension of credit, transferring to the lessee all responsibilities of ownership (maintenance, insurance, taxes) for a period of time closely approximating the useful life of the asset. At the end of the lease period, the asset may either be purchased by the lessee or returned to the lessor. An operating lease, on the other hand, does not involve an extension of credit or a long-term fixed commitment. Operating costs are generally borne by the lessor, who assumes the responsibilities and risk of ownership including risk of obsolescence.

## EVALUATING THE COST OF LEASING

The evaluation of the cost of a lease involves discounting a stream of after-tax cash flows as was indicated in Exhibit 5.1. Such discounting follows from the fact that the value of the future cash flows decreases with time.

Many of the methods for evaluating the cost of leasing have been proposed to resolve two basic issues in the lease/purchase decision:

1  Should the investment decision be separated from the financing decision?
2  What is the appropriate interest rate for discounting the component cash flows?

The answers to these two questions lie partly in the approach selected for the evaluation. One approach compares the net present values under each financing alternative, somewhat as we did in Exhibit 5.1. (Actually, we took the differences in the cash flows and discounted the difference.) Another approach compares the internal rate of return of the lease alternative with a criterion interest rate. (The internal rate of return is the interest rate that equates the present value of the future cash flows generated by an investment to the initial amount of the investment.) The arguments for and against each approach and the philosophy behind the methods presented within each approach are examined in the next section.

### The Financing Versus Investment Decision

In the theory of capital budgeting, it is accepted that financing and investment decisions should be separated. An investment should be evaluated on the basis of the cash flows it will generate relative to the amount of the investment. Once that evaluation has been made, the method of financing the investment is then determined. At any point in time, several investment projects are competing for a limited pool for funds, some of which are financed with debt, some with equity or internal cash flows, and still others with a combination financing plan such as leasing. Since managers are assumed to attempt to preserve some long run debt to equity ratio, the decision to finance one project with debt will presumably be counterbalanced with the decision to finance another project with equity. Attempting to correlate specific investments with specific financing plans, however, is not usually considered feasible. The problem with this theoretical framework when evaluating leases is that leasing is both a financing and an investment decision. The lessor is supplying both the use of the asset as well as the funds to acquire the asset and is charging for both. Also, initial investment in a lease is usually equal to zero, whereas the investment of funds in a purchase may equal 100 percent of the cost.

Under the conventional methods for lease analysis, which attempt to separate the investment and financing decision, the analyst typically compares the after-tax cash outflows under leasing with those of a cash purchase. This comparison implies that only the operating flows pertaining to the investment decision will be analyzed. However, since the cash outflows in the leasing alternative implicitly contain an interest element (due to the lack of an initial investment), a financing charge should be identified as part of the leasing cash outflows, which would then be compared to the outflows arising from a pure cash purchase. Unfortunately, including an interest element in the analysis on the lease side introduces an imputed cash flow, which distorts the analysis. However, the same problem would exist if a firm wished to purchase the asset on an installment basis. The firm could simply borrow the funds required, which borrowing then would allow the firm to obtain an interest deduction for tax purposes. It would still be necessary to input an interest charge on the lease side.

To compare the cost of leases with other methods of acquisition, it is necessary to distinguish between those cash flows that arise from the financing and those that arise from the investment (i.e., operating cash inflows and outflows). A loan can be assumed for the cash purchase price at the firm's incremental borrowing rate. The principal payments, as well as the after tax interest charges then would be discounted. The result then would be compared to the after-tax cash flows of leasing (see lines 7 and 12 in Exhibit 5.1).

## Choosing the Appropriate Discount Rate

Another major issue in lease analysis is choosing the appropriate discount rate. The rate chosen to discount the various cash flow components generally depends on one of two factors: (1) the approach for evaluating leases (comparison of net present values or comparison of the internal rates of return) and (2) the assumptions behind the assumed risk in each cash flow component.

When the approach chosen is to compare incremental cash flows, all cash flow components are discounted at the internal rate of return or the implicit rate in the lease, based on the assumption that all cash flows associated with the lease plan have the same cost to the company. The cash flows are compared with the cost of borrowed funds used to finance an equivalent purchase. On the other hand, when we compare net present values, we ordinarily discount the cash flows of greater certainty (contractual payments) at the firm's borrowing rate. Cash flows associated with operations (e.g., depreciation and interest expense) are usually discounted at the firm's after-tax cost of capital.

## A Framework for Lease Evaluation

The conventional approach for comparing present values starts by discounting the after-tax lease payments to find the cost of the lease, which is then compared with the purchase price of the asset less the discounted tax savings of depreciation. If the alternative to leasing is debt financing, the after-tax cash flows related to the payments are also discounted to arrive at the present value of the debt. Exhibit 5.1 illustrated the conventional method. One problem with this method is that by varying the amount or timing of the installment payments under the purchase alternative or under the lease alternative, the present value advantage of one or the other alternative can be altered.

In an attempt to resolve this problem, Richard F. Vancil proposed the Basic Interest Rate method whereby the lease payments are discounted at the firm's incremental borrowing rate.* By this means, the firm theoretically arrives at the present value of the amount of funds provided by the lease. The difference between the present value of the lease payments and the cash purchase price of the leased property is assumed to provide a premium to the lessor for risk assumption, costs associated with negotiating the lease, compensating balances or commitment fees required by lessor's bank, and lessor's borrowing costs. These costs would be borne by the lessee had it in fact obtained the loan itself. Therefore, to equate the lease alternative and the installment purchase alternative, the premium should be added as an additional imputed payment at the beginning of the lease. In Exhibit 5.1, since the present value of the lease payments, when discounted at the lessee's incremental borrowing rate, is equal to the cash purchase price, there is no lessor premium. Hence it is only the excess of the present value of depreciation and interest above the present value of rent that gives the advantage to ownership.

Another method of lease versus buy analysis that recognizes that a lease may require a premium to the lessor, in present value terms, over and above a cash purchase is that put forth by Bower, Herringer, and Williamson.** They assume

---

*Richard F. Vancil, "Lease or Borrow—New Method of Analysis," *Harvard Business Review* (September 1961).

**Richard S. Bower, Frank C. Herringer, and J. Peter Williamson, "Lease Evaluation," *The Accounting Review* (April 1966).

that the advantage or disadvantage of a lease versus a purchase can be expressed as the sum of the financial advantage or disadvantage (less amounts financed) and the operating advantage or disadvantage. This may be expressed mathematically as

$$L = \left[ C - \frac{Rn}{(1 + r)^n} \right] + \left[ \frac{t(Rn - Dn - In)}{(1 + i)^n} \right] \tag{1}$$

which may be rewritten as

$$L = \left[ C - \frac{tDn}{(1 + i)^n} - \frac{tIn}{(1 + i)^n} \right] - \left[ \frac{Rn}{(1 + r)^n} - \frac{tRn}{(1 + i)^n} \right] \tag{2}$$

where   $L$ = advantage or disadvantage of lease alternative
         $C$ = cash purchase price of leased asset
        $Dn$ = annual depreciation for year, $n = 1, 2, \ldots, N$
        $In$ = interest portion of lease or loan
        $Rn$ = total lease payment per year
         $t$ = marginal tax rate
         $i$ = firm's after-tax cost of capital
         $r$ = firm's incremental borrowing rate

All summations are from $n = 0$ to $n = N$.

Note that if the marginal tax rate is zero, then the advantage of the lease alternative is reduced to only the financial advantage, which is equal to the excess of the cash purchase price above the present value of the lease payments discounted at the firm's incremental borrowing rate.

Also note that if the cash purchase price $C$ is equal to the present value of the principal and interest payments required under an installment purchase, then equation (2) is a mathematical representation of Exhibit 5.1, excluding the effect of the investment tax credit.

The effect of the investment tax credit could be introduced by setting $C$ equal to the cash purchase price less the investment tax credit realizable by the lessee.

If the advantage of leasing $L$ is set equal to zero and the expression is rearranged to solve for the marginal tax rate $t$, the result is:

$$t = \frac{Rn/(1 + r)^n - C}{(Rn - Dn - In)/(1 + i)^n} \tag{3}$$

This may be called the break-even tax rate. Effective tax rates greater than the break-even rate would indicate a preference for owning over leasing.

In this expression it can be seen that when the present value of the lease payments discounted at the incremental borrowing rate is equal to the cash purchase price of the asset, the break-even tax rate is equal to zero. This means that at any positive effective tax rate, there would be a preference toward owning. If the firm did not pay taxes there would be an indifference between leasing and owning.

If the present value of the lease payments, $Rn/(1 + r)^n$, is less than the cash purchase price, or, alternatively, less than the present value of the principal and interest payments under an installment loan, then there can be a positive break-even tax rate. The solution to the break-even tax rate is dependent on the extent of the excess of the present value of depreciation and interest payments above the present value of the rent (i.e., the denominator of the break-even formula.) This excess is, in turn, dependent on the use of accelerated or straight line methods of depreciation.

If expression (3) is rearranged and solved for $Rn$, we have

$$\sum \frac{Rn}{(1 + r)^n} - \sum \frac{tRn}{(1 + i)^n} = C - t \sum \frac{Dn + In}{(1 + i)^n} \qquad (4)$$

Then if we let $r = i$ and assume that all $Rn$ are equal (i.e., a level rent),

$$(1 - t) Rn \sum \frac{1}{(1 + i)^n} = C - t \sum \frac{Dn + In}{(1 + i)^n} \qquad (5)$$

and

$$Rn = \frac{C - t \sum (Dn + In)/(1 + i)^n}{(1 - t) \sum 1/(1 + i)^n} \qquad (6)$$

which indicates that the rent at which a firm should be indifferent to the advantages of leasing versus owning is equal to the cash price less the present value of the tax benefits of owning divided by one minus the tax rate (in order to obtain a pre-tax rent) divided by the present value of an annuity of $n$ payments of $1 discounted at $i$ interest rate. Again, of course, the break-even rent is dependent on the tax rate and the method of depreciation.

## Conclusion

Evaluating the cost of a lease financing arrangement depends on whether the investment decision and the financing decision should be separated and on the appropriate rates for discounting cash flows. Two approaches have been identified for answering these questions: comparing present value costs and comparing the rates of return on incremental cash flows. In either approach, the cash flow under the conventional financing arrangement must be adjusted for comparability with the lease financing arrangement since lease payments often contain charges for services provided in excess of the actual financing. The difficulty in resolving the various methods stems from the fact that lease financing is both a financing decision and an investment decision. Attempts to resolve the problem, or to separate the decision, will probably be less than optimal.

# Chapter 6

# EQUIPMENT LEASE FINANCING

Equipment leasing is actually an unusual method of business asset acquisition. Except for a few industries, such as railroads and airlines, and certain types of equipment, such as computers, equipment is usually financed as part of the overall capital requirements of a business, along with plant, inventory, receivables, and working capital. The capital required for business assets is usually drawn from three sources: debt securities, equity securities, and internally generated funds.

In recent years, a number of financing alternatives for equipment have developed. Most of these involve some form of lease financing. Examples include industrial development bonds, pollution control equipment financing, Title XI guarantees under the Federal Merchant Marine Act, and other governmental incentive programs.

The increasing popularity of lease financing techniques is attributable to the advantages that they can offer compared to conventional financing. The most significant advantage that an equipment lease financing is likely to offer is a lower cost of funds. Even without a cost-of-funds advantage, a particular lease financing may be the best method of financing equipment costs for a particular user. However, a lease financing can involve difficulties that outweigh savings in the cost of funds.

It is important that managers, accountants, and attorneys develop the ability to evaluate equipment lease financing proposals. Once lease financing is selected as the preferred financing technique, the manager should be alert to factors that will ensure that the financing is planned, negotiated, and executed to the best advantage of the business. In carrying out these functions, the manager will call on the services of legal counsel, accountants, financial consultants, engineering and operating personnel, and other specialized advisors.

The feasibility of an equipment lease must be determined before proceeding with further analysis of the lease. Feasibility should be questioned in several areas: (1) feasibility under the lessee's corporate indentures and other credit documents, (2) feasibility under regulatory considerations peculiar to the lessee or the equipment, and (3) feasibility of the equipment itself. When the equipment has already been ordered, the terms of the purchase contract may also affect the feasibility of lease financing.     The lessee's existing bond indentures and similar debt agreements should be reviewed for provisions that may affect a lease. In some cases, a bond indenture will contain a prohibition against equipment lease financing. Such provisions are not common, but are appearing more frequently, particularly in term loan and revolving credit agreements. Corporate charter provisions may contain prohibitions or limitations on lease financing. After-acquired property clauses, which are found in many corporate bond indentures, can be difficult, particularly if the provisions for removal of property from the lien of the indenture are stringent. If the prospective lessee has title to the equipment, these after-acquired clauses, may make it difficult to assure clear title to the equipment for the lessor and prevent the security of a first lien for other investors in the lease financing. Convenants contained in debt instruments should be reviewed to be sure that the execution of a proposed lease does not render the lessee unable to satisfy a covenant. For example, a covenant to maintain, own, and operate a complete and fully equipped manufacturing facility at all times may preclude a lease of some essential production equipment. Another matter to be considered is that equipment financed through a lease does not normally qualify as a bondable property addition. Therefore, the equipment cannot be used as the basis for a future bond issue. This is reasonable, since the leased equipment does not represent any additional invested capital of the lessee or security for the lessee's bondholders.

Another limitation on the ability of business to engage in lease financing is the regulatory requirements to which the prospective lessee or the equipment itself may be subject. There are few industries or categories of equipment that are not encumbered by laws, regulations, and restrictions. A procedure to identify possible problems in this area is to consider whether the proposed lease financing involves a person, a transaction, a security, or a type of equipment that requires a special governmental license, approval or consent and, if so, whether such license, approval, or consent will be difficult or impossible to obtain, or whether the required license, approval, or consent must be obtained by the lessor or other investor in the financing. It may be discovered that the passive ownership of the leased equipment will subject the lessor to regulation or eligibility requirements that are unacceptable or cannot be met. Alternatively, the proposed financing may be deemed to involve the issuance of a security by a party whose security issues require prior government approval that is unobtainable. For example, a lessor of utility property may be deemed to be a utility, thus requiring regulation by a Public Utilities Commission.

Problems may also be encountered with equipment purchase contracts, if they have been executed prior to the lease financing. Two troublesome provisions are those for progress payments in advance of delivery and for passage of title from the supplier prior to delivery. Progress payments are a problem because the lease financing investors are often unwilling to advance funds before the completed equipment has been delivered and accepted by the lessee. Passage of title prior to delivery can be a problem because it may result in vesting title to the equipment in the lessee, thereby creating indenture lien problems and possibly raising uncertainties as to whether the equipment, when retransferred to the lessor, will still be considered new equipment for purposes of qualifying for tax benefits. Planning for the equipment lease should begin prior to equipment acquisition, so that these problems can be avoided. An equipment purchase contract problem that may not be avoidable, even with the advance planning, is multiple deliveries, because such delivery schedules are frequently dictated by the requirements of the lessee's business. When the equipment is to be delivered in separate transactions over a long period, separate closings may be required. It may not be feasible to negotiate for flexibility in the investors' commitments.

Finally, obstacles to a successful equipment lease financing may arise from the nature of the equipment itself. In an equipment lease, the following suggestions should be noted.

The equipment should be new. If the equipment is not new, it may not qualify for the favorable tax credit and accelerated depreciation treatments that are generally the purpose of a lease financing.

The equipment should be durable. If the equipment has only a short estimated useful life, it may fail to satisfy tax and accounting criteria.

It should not be subject to rapid obsolescence. If the equipment is likely to become obsolete within a short time, an equipment lease may require the lessee to use outmoded equipment.

Maintenance requirements should not be great. If the equipment requires frequent modifications, additions, or repairs, a lease financing may be uneconomical because the largest amount of equipment costs may not be in the original cost financed under the lease, but in the lessee's subsequent alterations.

The equipment should be movable. If it is uneconomical or otherwise impracticable to remove the equipment from the prospective lessee's site, it may be difficult to treat the transaction as a lease.

It should be marketable. If there is no market for the equipment because, for example, it is uniquely adapted to the lessee's needs, the equipment may lack the residual value necessary to qualify the transaction as a lease.

The equipment should consist of a discrete unit. If the equipment lacks sharply defined and readily identifiable boundaries or consists of many different elements, it will be difficult to lease. An example would be the pipes, pumps, valves, sensors, wiring, and controls that make up a fire detection and control system for a large building. Equipment of this nature not only raises questions as to residual value (since the cost of removal is likely to exceed resale value), but also presents administrative problems in identifying the component parts under lease and complying with maintenance, insurance, and similar lease covenants.

The equipment should be readily identifiable. If the equipment consists of units that are interchangeable with the identical to other units with which they may be commingled, administrative problems may arise unless there is some convenient method, such as serial numbers, to identify the units under lease.

The equipment also should be relatively expensive. If the leased equipment has a low unit cost, the ratio of administrative costs to potential cost-of-funds savings is likely to be less favorable, all other things being equal, because administrative costs tend to rise with the number of units.

An equipment lease may be feasible even if the equipment lacks some of the preceding characteristics, but if it lacks these characteristics to any substantial extent, a lease financing is probably not feasible.

## COST

Once the business manager has determined that a proposed equipment lease is feasible, his next consideration should be an analysis of the cost of the proposed lease. Normally, the prospective lessee is seeking, and expects to enjoy, a savings in the cost compared to alternative methods of financing the equipment. The lessee should be careful that the saving is not illusory because of indirect costs inherent in an equipment lease. It is essential to compare the proposed equipment lease with alternative financing methods on a present-value basis. (See Chapter 5.)

One significant indirect cost to the lessee is the surrender of the residual value of the equipment. If the lessee anticipates having to replace the equipment at the end of the lease term, the present value of the cost of such replacement must be taken into consideration in determining the real cost of the financing. On the other hand, if the lessee anticipates that it will have no need for such equipment at the end of the lease term, or that the equipment will in fact have no residual value, this will affect the decision in a different way.

In addition to residual value, the lessee is surrendering other benefits of ownership. The foremost of these are investment tax credits and accelerated depreciation, the collateral value of the equipment as a basis for raising additional capital, and, in the case of regulated industries, the rate base. The value accorded each factor by the lessee will vary widely from company to company. For example, a lessee with substantial loss carryforwards may place little or no value on the tax credits and depreciation deductions being given up.

Another factor that can affect the lessee's cost of funds is the fees of the parties involved in an equipment lease. These include fees (lessee's, lessor's, lenders', trustees', equipment supplier's, local and special—such as bond or maritime), placement fees, trustees' fees, printing costs, and the costs of continuing compliance with various lease covenants, for example, the costs of providing legal opinions and auditors' certificates. These costs can be quite substantial—counsel fees alone for a complex lease financing can exceed $100,000. There should be clear agreement in advance as to how these costs are to be distributed.

Incidental costs that are inherent in a lease financing should also be considered. For example, the lessee may incur sales or excise taxes that might have been avoided except for the lease. The lessee may have to bear the cost of organizing and maintaining a special subsidiary for the purpose of the financing. There may be some loss of economies of scale if separate maintenance or insurance provisions are required for the leased equipment. Also, any continuing expenses that the lessee may be required to reimburse to other parties should be taken into account.

Apart from the comparative costs of funds, several other factors should be considered in assessing the relative merits of a lease financing. These include the impact on the lessee's credit, reported earnings, cash flow, and tax positon, the required lead time, questions of flexibility and other matters, and the risks to which the lessee may be exposed.

Probably the most important equipment leasing consideration for the lessee, after the cost of funds, is the impact of the proposed equipment lease on the lessee's ability to raise other funds.

One of the frequently cited advantages of lease financing is its off-balance-sheet character; that is, it is financing that does not appear on the face of the lessee's balance sheet. This advantage has been much overstated, and developments in lease accounting have largely eliminated off-balance-sheet treatment for major equipment leases. In addition, investors, creditors, and security analysts are aware of the necessity of considering any substantial lease financing obligations in assessing the lessee's credit.

In addition to the balance-sheet considerations, there are other ways in which an equipment lease may affect the lessee's ability to raise additional capital. The fixed-charges coverage ratios that some companies show in their SEC filings may be affected differently by similar amounts of conventional debt and lease financing. However, this effect is limited by the SEC's requirement that a portion of rental payments be included in computing fixed charge ratios. More significant is the impact that an equipment lease may have on the interest coverage ratio computed under the lessee's bond indenture. Here there may be a great variance in effect, with the lessee showing a higher ratio (and, therefore, higher bonding ability) under a lease financing than under a comparable debt financing.

Another effect on the lessee's credit may arise from the views of rating agencies, securities analysts, and the lessee's bankers as to the appropriate relationship that the lessee should maintain between lease financing and conventional debt and equity financing. A prospective lessee should consult these sources to determine their reactions to any substantial amount of lease financing.

Another consideration is the role of equipment leasing as a supplementary source of financing. Whenever a company is engaged in an extensive capital additions program, the company may find that even though its credit is recognized as sound, there is a limit to the amount of securities that can be absorbed by the conventional capital markets within a limited time. In this event, lease financing can prove to be useful source of additional capital. This consideration may make equipment leasing attractive even in the absence of a cost-of-funds advantage.

Another factor that the prospective lessee should review is the impact of the proposed lease on the company's cash flow and reported earnings. Even if the aggregate cash and earning effects are expected to equivalent to a comparable amount of conventional financing, the differences in timing may be significant to the user.

The lessee should also consider the impact of the proposed lease on the lessee's tax position. As discussed in a previous chapter, lease financing is attractive to a lessee in a net loss carryforward position, to a lessee with substantial tax credit carryforwards, or when a period of losses or low income years is anticipated. In each such case, the lessee would be trading off tax shelter (i.e., the tax benefits of ownership) that has little or no value to it in exchange for a reduction in its direct cost of funds. A similar consideration is presented to a public utility or other regulated company if the regulatory authorities require that tax-shelter benefits flow through to the public. Another aspect of tax effects is that lease financing will result in a change in the identity of the purchaser and owner of the equipment that may have sales tax and property tax consequences if either the lessee or the lessor has tax-exempt status or is subject to a special rate.

With regard to nonfinancial matters, one of the factors that should be carefully considered is the greater lead time generally required to put lease financing in place compared to that required for conventional financing. Greater time is required because of the complexity of this type of financing, many parties and because of the fact that a lease financing tends to be a transaction involving many negotiated issues. If the company's operational requirements for the equipment do not allow the necessary time, it may be preferable to seek a different financing format.

Another nonfinancial, but important, consideration is the matter of flexibility. By its nature, a lease financing leaves the company less free than an owner would be in dealing with the equipment. A lessee's assessment of a proposed lease is based on the assumption that the lessee will have need of, and will be able to use, the equipment throughout the lease term. If the need for, or the ability to use, the equipment ceases to exist, a previously favorable arrangement may become unfavorable. Similarly, as a result of a change in conditions during the lease term, initially acceptable lease covenants may force a lessee to incur unexpected costs. Therefore, it is important that the lessee consider what flexibility the proposed lease gives in the event that unforeseen developments make the lease unfavorable.

An additional aspect that the prospective lessee should consider is the managerial commitment inherent in a lease financing. In the initial stages, the lessee must be prepared to involve its legal, accounting, financial personnel and operating staff. The operating personnel are often the only ones qualified to evaluate the reasonableness and cost of the obligations that the lease will impose on the lessee. After the lease is in place, continuing involvement by legal, accounting, financial, and operating personnel is essential to assure compliance with the lessee's covenants as to maintenance, recordkeeping, uniform commercial code (UCC) filings, and other matters. Furthermore, if unforeseen developments require renegotiation of the original terms, substantial involvement by the lessee's management may again be required.

The impact of a proposed lease financing on the lessee's relationship with the equipment supplier should also be considered. It is often necessary to obtain the cooperation of the equipment supplier in structuring the lease financing, particularly if the equipment purchase contract has already been signed and if the contract was not drawn to accommodate the proposed lease financing. Suppliers are usually cooperative, since the object of the financing is to provide them with payment. However, such cooperation may carry a price, which is reflected in the cost of the equipment or other terms of the contract.

If the equipment user is in a regulated industry, additional considerations may come into play as the proposed lease financing wends its way through the regulatory agencies to which the user is subject. Two examples mentioned previously are the impact on rate base assets and the effect of flow-through treatment of accelerated depreciation and investment tax credits. A further point is the effect of leasing on the rate of capital recovery. If equipment is purchased by a regulated user, this investment is normally recovered through depreciation allowances, but at rates that are often considered by the users to be too slow. In contrast, if the same equipment is leased, the user's investment is recovered immediately, through allowance of the company's rental payments as operating expenses.

## PLANNING LEASE FINANCING ARRANGEMENTS

Planning for lease financing should begin before acquisition of the property, since problems are often created or avoided at this point.

The prospective lessee should see to it that the equipment purchase contract authorizes assignment of the purchase contract to permit the prospective lessor to acquire the equipment directly from the supplier, with the warranties and other rights that the lessee would have had as buyer. The contract should provide for consent on the part of the vendor to the assignment to the lessor, confirming the lessor's rights under the purchase contract. Provisions regarding passage of title should be structured to avoid problems under the lessee's bond indenture, to minimize sales and use taxes, and to satisfy applicable income tax requirements so as to assure the lessor of any anticipated tax benefits. Also, the delivery and payment schedules should be coordinated with the times the lessor and other lease financing investors expect to make their investments. Since the lessee will normally receive no warranties with respect to the equipment from the lessor, the equipment purchase contract should permit enforcement of the supplier's warranties by the lessee. The prospective lessee should also attempt to provide in the equipment purchase contract for the cooperation of the equipment supplier in consummating the lease financing. For example, the lessee should seek the supplier's agreement to provide to the lessor such representations, certificates, title documents, and legal opinions as the lessor may require. In some cases, the lessor will request an agreement with the supplier concerning these matters. It may be feasible to provide for such agreement in the equipment purchase contract.

If the vendor requires progress payments, the prospective lessee must arrange for interim financing, unless it is feasible for the lessee to advance these payments out of working capital funds.

The prospective lessee's legal counsel should pay particular attention to securities law considerations affecting the lessee and to regulatory approvals and tax rulings. The lessee's counsel should be aware that, for securities law purposes, the lessee may be considered the issuer of any securities that may be issued in connection with the lease. This is due to the fact that, regardless of the form of the transaction, it is essentially based on the lessee's credit. Therefore, the lessee's counsel should review the proposed offering procedures whereby investors in the proposed lease will be solicited. Normally, the private offering exemption from the registration requirements of the Federal Securities Act will be relied on, and care must be taken to ensure that the offering procedures qualify for this exemption. During the planning stage, the lessee's counsel should compile a list of all required tax rulings and regulatory or other governmental approvals. These often involve substantial lead times. For local tax rulings and regulatory approvals uniquely associated with the lessee or its industry, the other parties will generally look to the lessee's counsel for guidance.

Review of the proposed lease by the lessee's accounting staff and its outside auditors should not be overlooked. To avoid serious problems, the lessee's management should have a clear understanding of the accounting treatment the transaction will receive and changes in treatment that may be required in the future. Also, the accountants and outside auditors should be consulted as to the feasibility and cost of any accountants' or auditors' certificates required by the lease financing documents.

A point that should be borne in mind from the outset of discussions concerning a lease financing is the matter of expenses. Although the expenses of all parties are in theory borne by the lessee through its rental payments, even if they are not paid directly by the lessee, in practice it is preferable for each party to bear its own expenses. This not only tends to keep down the total expenses, but protects the prospective lessee in the event that the transaction is not consummated. However, printing costs are almost always paid by the lessee directly. It should be made clear at the outset that the printer will be selected by the lessee and that no copy or work orders will be sent to the printer until approved by the lessee so that extensive overtime and resetting costs can be avoided.

Finally, a useful tool in planning and preparing for the negotiation of an equipment lease is a review of documents from similar prior lease financing transactions. These can be obtained from a number of sources, but the most convenient are probably legal counsel, industry associations, and equipment lease brokers.

The documentation of a lease financing is complex and involves many negotiated terms. Although no two lease financings are identical, many of their points are similar, regardless of the form of the documents. The following are some terms that should be considered by the lessee. The lessee's representatives should be clear about their objectives with respect to these points before entering the negotiation of the lease financing arrangement.

The lessee should attempt to retain maximum freedom to amend the equipment purchase contract and to revise the specifications of the equipment to be delivered.

The lessee should attempt to retain, under the lease financing documents, not only the right to proceed directly against the supplier with respect to warranties, refunds, price adjustments, and other claims arising from the equipment purchase contract, but also the right to retain any recovery, unless the lease financing document otherwise makes the lessee whole.

The prospective lessee's right to reassignment of the equipment purchase contract in the event that the lease is not consummated should be stated definitely.

The lessee should consider whether the protection of its interests requires any restrictions on transfer of the lessor's interest in the transaction or in the equipment. For example, the lessor's interests should only be transferred to other financial institutions.

The lessee should set closing conditions that provide maximum flexibility. There is often a substantial lapse of time between the execution of the lease financing documents and the date of the closing. Changed circumstances may make it impossible to satisfy elaborate closing conditions. Therefore, workable procedures should be provided whereby such conditions can be waived or modified. This is important when there are a large number of investors in the transaction. The consequences of an inability to satisfy a closing condition should be considered thoroughly.

The lessee should review the impact of a failure to consummate, or a premature termination of, the lease, through the fault of a party other than the lessee. For example, loss of the tax benefits of ownership of new equipment may result, and the lessee may be obligated to indemnify other parties. The lessee should seek provisions that protect it against such consequences.

Often equipment lease financing documents will require the lessee to indemnify the other parties to the financing against various risks and expenses. For the most part, these risks and expenses are those normally associated with the ownership and operation of the leased property, for example, property taxes, license fees, and liability. The indemnities ordinarily do not increase the exposure of the lessee beyond what it would be if the lessee owned the property. However, other indemnities may increase the lessee's exposure to liability beyond what it would have been had the lessee purchased the equipment. Indemnifying other parties against unexpected income tax liabilities can be hazardous. Such an indemnity may include a grossing up provision, which requires the indemnitor to make the indemnitee whole, net of taxes on the indemnity payment. Thus the indemnification can cost the lessee more than it benefits the part indemnified. The lessee should review the scope of such obligations and the extent to which they can be assumed prudently.

Provisions should be made for the allocation of the interests in claims against third parties, including tax refund claims, in respect to the leased property. Although it may be equitable for the lessor to share in, or enjoy entirely, the proceeds of such a claim, in most cases such claims will be compensatory for a loss suffered by the lessee and therefore the lease financing documents should protect the rights of the lessee to such proceeds. Also, the lease financing documents authorize the lessee to sue and take other action in the name of the lessor when necessary.

Typically, a lease financing will have a term at least several years. Over a period of years changing circumstances may make amendments to the lease desirable. The lease should contain procedures for the negotiation and execution of amendments. As in the case of waiver of closing conditions, this is critical when there are many investors in the lease financing. In this regard, it is helpful if the lease financing documents include the appointment of a lead investor with authority to consent to amendments on behalf of all investors of the same class (i.e., a lead lender or lead equity investor).

Since the lessee will be paying the fees of any trustees to be appointed in connection with the equipment lease financing, the lessee should insist on the right to select the initial trustee and any successor trustee. This is of interest to the lessee because the fees of institutional trustees may vary considerably. Frequently a considerable savings can be obtained through competitive fee quotations.

The lessee should give particular attention to the circumstances under which the lease financing documents permit a premature termination. It is common to provide for a termination in the event of physical destruction or loss of equipment. Typically, the lease financing documents will provide that in the event of loss or destruction the lessee will make a lump-sum termination payment calculated to make the lessor whole. The extent to which such payments will include all or a portion of the lessor's anticipated profit is a matter for negotiation between the lessor and the lessee at the time the lease financing documents are drafted. In addition to physical damage to or destruction of the equipment, the lessee may wish to provide for other events that will prematurely terminate the lease and trigger a required termination payment to the lessor. Examples of such events might be technological or economic obsolescense of the equipment, imposition of environment or other restrictions that make continued use of the equipment uneconomic or illegal, or other events that make continued use of the equipment by the lessee inpracticable.

## Purchase and Renewal Options

Provisions for purchase and renewal options in lease financing arrangements are circumscribed by the criteria for recognition of the transaction as a true lease for tax purposes. However, within these limitations purchase or renewal options can significantly enhance the attractiveness of the lease financing arrangement to the lessee. The lessee should be alert to the timing and notice requirements incorporated in such options. Particularly if the option requires negotiation of an agreed purchase price or renewal rental, the option procedures should leave the lessee sufficient time to look elsewhere for replacement equipment if such negotiations prove unsatisfactory.

## Insurance Covenants

The lessee will be required to maintain property damage and liability insurance with respect to the equipment for the benefit of the lessor. The lessee should be certain that such covenants are compatible with the lessee's own insurance program and that they do not obligate the lessee to provide coverage that is unobtainable or unreasonably expensive. If the lessor demands a level of insurance beyond the lessee's normal insurance program, the lessee should make sure that the higher level of insurance on the leased equipment will not trigger a provision in some other agreement by which the lessee is bound that would force the lessee to raise its general level of insurance. Covenants for loss-payable and notification endorsements should be cleared with the lessee's insurance specialists to be certain that such endorsements are obtainable and that they will in fact be obtained and continued through successive renewals of policies. If the lessee self-insures to some extent, the lease financing documents permit the lessee to self-insure the leased property to the same degree. If the value of the leased property is insignificant in comparison to the net worth of the lessee, consideration should be given to dispensing with insurance covenants as long as the lessee maintains a stated level of net worth.

If the value of the leased equipment is significant, the lease financing documents specify the extent to which the lessee is responsible for the costs of delivering the equipment to the lessor on termination of the lease. Matters to be considered include dismantling costs, packing costs, shipping and insurance costs, place of delivery, storage arrangements, risk of loss, abandonment privileges, and termination of the lessee's responsibility for the equipment.

A lease financing agreement will require the lessee to furnish to the lessor periodic reports, certificates, and sometimes legal and accounting opinions with respect to the status, condition, location, and inspection of the equipment, compliance with covenants, and the financial condition of the lessee. These covenants should be carefully reviewed with the personnel who will be responsible for complying with such covenants to ensure that such compliance is feasible and will be carried out.

As noted earlier, the lease financing documents should provide for the assignment of responsibility for both initial and continuing expenses of the transaction.

Lease financing is an attractive supplement to conventional financing. Its employment requires both an evaluation of the lease financing documents and careful planning for the factors that contribute to a successful lease financing.

## Chapter 7

# SALE-LEASEBACKS IN REAL ESTATE

Recently, interest rates have become volatile and unpredictable. A result of this turbulence has been the disturbance of credit and equity markets and difficulty for corporate officers, whose task it is to plan the cash needs of their corporations. Many corporations have found the equity markets to be closed, and many have not been able to raise cash at any price and therefore have had to abandon plans for expansion and capital replacements. During this period, an overlooked method of raising cash on advantageous terms is the sale-leaseback.

Companies often carry as fixed assets on their balance sheets a substantial amount of real estate that may have a higher value than the amount at which such assets are carried on the books. By selling and leasing back such assets to an entity that can obtain tax benefits and/or potential long-term appreciation from the property, a company may generate cash. Financial officers and their legal advisors should approach sale-leasebacks in real estate with an understanding of the business alternatives, as well as an understanding of the tax considerations that affect the structuring of a sale-leaseback transaction.

A sale-leaseback entails the sale and simultaneous leaseback of real property for a period of years. The lease will generally provide that the return to the lessor (buyer) will be net. That means that the lessee will pay all expenses of operating the facility, including insurance, maintenance, and taxes.

The principal advantage to the seller-lessee in a sale-leaseback transaction is that it is a less expensive way of raising funds.

Utilities in particular are in constant need of funds to finance their increasing capital expenditure requirements. Traditionally, utilities have been reluctant to use sale-leasebacks because of concern regarding a reduction of their rate base. However, rate base is not as important as it formerly was because of the large expenditures for fixed assets, such as nuclear power plants, which are included in rate base. Liquidity is now more important, and, with increasing frequency, utilities are utilizing sale-leasebacks.

Another advantage of sale-leasebacks is that, for accounting purposes, a lease may improve the balance sheet of the seller-lessee in that the lease is not reflected as a liability in the financial statements. Other advantages to the seller-lessee include:

1 Avoidance of restrictive covenants in bank agreements and loan indentures that do not preclude a company's ability to lease property but may preclude the expenditure of funds for an outright purchase.

2 Avoidance of usury limitations in states where an outright loan might be deemed usurious, but where a lease, not being considered a loan, would not be similarly affected.

3 Passing on to the buyer-lessor the uncertainties of residual value where the buyer-lessor may be willing to take this risk because of the other tax benefits it may be obtaining.

The essential aspect of sale-leasebacks is, however, the ultimate cost of the transaction. For the company that does not have access to the public debt or equity markets, the only alternative to a sale-leaseback is mortgage financing.

A purchaser-lessor in a sale-leaseback transaction will look ultimately to the mortgage market as his source of funds. A purchaser-lessor may be in a stronger position to obtain mortgage financing than the seller-lessee because the lender (mortgagee) has another layer of protection in the event the seller-lessee fails financially (i.e., the purchaser-lessor, in order to protect its equity investment, will continue to pay the lender while it looks to replace the financially strained seller-lessee). As a result of this added security, a lender may agree to make a loan that it would otherwise reject or perhaps give the purchaser-lessor a more favorable rate of interest than it would give the lessee if the lessee were the direct owner-mortgagor.

Another advantage of a sale-leaseback over mortgage financing is that the sale-leaseback is capable of generating funds up to 100 percent of the fair market value of the facility. Most institutional real estate mortgages are limited to 75 to 80 percent of fair market value.

In a sale-leaseback, rental payments represent repayment of the sales price of the property to the purchaser-lessor plus some element of return on the investment comparable to the payment of interest and principal under a mortgage. In a true lease situation, all payments made by the lessee are deductible as rent. On a mortgage, the mortgagor can only deduct the interest element of its mortgage payment and is denied a deduction for the principal portion, which increases each year as the interest payment declines. The mortgagor does, however, retain the ability to depreciate the property and to realize the residual value of the property at the end of the mortgage term.

An analysis of the comparative costs between a sale-leaseback and mortgage financing should include factors such as the current and prospective tax rates, available depreciation deductions and methods, tax gain or loss on the transaction, rates of interest, and an estimate of the future residual value of the property at the expiration of the lease term.

Assume a $12 million facility that Hero Manufacturing Corporation, a 46 percent bracket taxpayer, has just purchased that includes land with a $2 million cost, a 30 year economic life, and an anticipated residual value at the end of 25 years of $6 million. The following analysis can be made comparing a 100 percent mortgage at 10 percent interest, self-liquidating over a 25 year period (payments monthly in arrears) with a 25 year sale-leaseback where the annual rent payments (also made monthly in arrears) are equal to the total debt service of the mortgage. The leaseback will generate the same after-tax cost each year:

## Leaseback

| | |
|---|---|
| Rent | $1,308,529 |
| Less tax savings | 601,923 |
| After-tax cost | $ 706,606 |

The mortgage will generate increasing after-tax costs each year, as seen in Exhibit 7.1.

To make an analysis of mortgage costs versus sale-leaseback cost, one must take the present value of the stream of after-tax costs of the mortgage alternative and compare this present value with the present value of the after-tax sale-leaseback costs, adding to the latter the present value of the expected value of the property at the end of the lease. If we assume a discount rate of 10 percent after tax, the approximate present value costs for the sale-leaseback would be $6,911,529 compared with a cost of $5,840,879 for the mortgage. An estimated residual value of zero would make a difference in the outcome of the analysis. Similarly, a difference would result if accelerated rather than straight line depreciation were used. As discussed in a previous chapter, the corporate tax rate plays a significant role in the analysis. The purpose of the preceding illustration is to show a method of analysis rather than to draw a conclusion as to the comparable costs. The length of mortgage and lease term, renewal options, purchase options, cost of money, and changes in tax rates should also be considered.

Corporations often are reluctant to sell property in a sale-leaseback at a price in excess of book carrying value because the gain thus triggered, absent depreciation recapture, will normally be taxed as a capital gain. The payment of tax on the gain will raise the effective cost to the seller-lessee unless the lessee has losses to utilize against the gains. If this tax gain can be offset by losses, it will

**Exhibit 7.1**  *After-Tax Costs of the Mortgage Alternative*

| Year | Mortgage | | |
|---|---|---|---|
| 1 | Total payment | | $1,308,529 |
| | Interest deduction | $1,194,885 | |
| | Depreciation (straight line) | 400,000 | |
| | (25 year life) | $1,594,885 | |
| | Tax savings | | 733,647 |
| | After-tax cost | | $ 574,882 |
| 5 | Total payment | | $1,308,529 |
| | Interest deduction | $1,139,273 | |
| | Depreciation deduction | 400,000 | |
| | | $1,539,273 | |
| | Tax savings | | 708,065 |
| | After-tax cost | | $ 600,464 |
| 10 | Total payment | | $1,308,529 |
| | Interest deduction | $1,030,050 | |
| | Depreciation deduction | 400,000 | |
| | | $1,430,050 | |
| | Tax savings | | $ 657,823 |
| | After-tax cost | | $ 650,706 |
| 15 | Total payment | | $1,308,529 |
| | Interest deduction | $ 850,345 | |
| | Depreciation deduction | 400,000 | |
| | | $1,250,345 | |
| | Tax savings | | $ 575,159 |
| | After-tax cost | | $ 733,370 |
| 20 | Total payment | | $1,308,529 |
| | Interest deduction | $ 554,675 | |
| | Depreciation deduction | 400,000 | |
| | | $ 954,675 | |
| | Tax savings | | $ 439,151 |
| | After-tax cost | | $ 869,378 |
| 25 | Total payment | | $1,308,529 |
| | Interest deduction | $ 185,773 | |
| | Depreciation deduction | 400,000 | |
| | | $ 585,773 | |
| | Tax savings | | 269,456 |
| | After-tax cost | | $1,039,073 |

generally be advantageous for the seller-lessee to sell at full fair market value. It should be noted that for accounting purposes any gain realized may not be reported except over the life of the lease.

Some corporations, notably bank holding companies, have a tax basis for real property that is greater than its fair market value. By selling and leasing back such property, a double advantage may be realized: a loss for tax purposes and no loss for accounting purposes except one that will be picked up gradually over the life of the lease.

## INSTALLMENT SALES

A seller-lessee may be able to sell real estate at a gain and avoid paying the tax in the year of sale by utilizing Section 453 of the Internal Revenue Code, which governs installment sales. Ordinarily a sale-leaseback would not be eligible for installment sale treatment since a seller sells the real estate for all cash and simultaneously leases it back. Assuming that mortgage money is available and the prospective seller-lessee first mortgages the property in anticipation of a sale and later sells and then leases back the property, the mortgage will not be considered cash received in the year of sale. However, the IRS might argue that the presale mortgage has no business purpose or is a sham, thereby resulting in the mortgage being treated as the equivalent of cash received in the year of sale. If the actual cash received is less than 30 percent of the selling price (i.e., cash plus the mortgage subject to which the property is being taken), then installment sale treatment may be obtained. To the extent that the mortgage exceeds the seller's tax basis in the property, the seller will be deemed to have received the equivalent of cash in the year of sale to the extent of such excess.

Mortgaging of the property may also be used where the seller-lessee wishes to take back a purchase-money mortgage as a portion of the consideration to be received.

When interest rates are high, some corporations may find the sale-leaseback market, as well as the mortgage and other long-term money markets, closed.

The sale-leaseback route may also be unavailable when a corporation with weak credit wishes to sell and lease back a number of small real estate sites for nonprime uses, for example, fast-food restaurants or gasoline stations. In these situations, a way open to a prospective seller-lessee for raising money is to take back a purchase-money mortgage in a sale-leaseback transaction. The buyer-lessor pays between 20 and 30 percent cash on the total selling price and the remaining portion of the selling price is provided by the seller taking back a purchase-money mortgage. The seller-lessee thus obtains cash immediately and can discount the purchase money mortgage at some point in the future when mortgage money is more readily available. As previously noted, the presence of a third party's equity in the property makes the purchase-money mortgage more marketable than it would be if the seller-lessee itself was the owner of the property.

This comes about because the rent the seller-lessee is paying is sufficient to give the buyer-lessor some return on his money plus an amount necessary to cover the debt service. The net result is that the seller-lessee will generate a tax deduction that will exceed the net amount of cash out of pocket. The point can be best illustrated by an example.

Hero Manufacturing Corporation sells and leases back property to Overload Systems for a total of $5 million; Overload puts up $1 million in cash, and Hero takes back a purchase-money mortgage of $4 million at an interest rate of 10 percent self-liquidating over the 25 year lease term, with annual payments totaling $440,672. The total annual rent is $540,672, which is sufficient to cover the debt service and give Overload a 10 percent ($100,000) return on its $1 million equity. Since Hero is getting back $440,672 of its $540,672 rent payment, it is only out of pocket $100,000 each year. However, because of the amortization factor inherent in the mortgage Hero gets a tax deduction for rent of $540,672 and income the first year of $400,000 interest plus a tax-free return of principal of $40,672. Accordingly, the first year's tax loss is $140,672 ($540,672–400,000) which is $40,672 larger than the $100,000 cash that the corporation was net out of pocket. Over the 25 year lease term, the corporation's out-of-pocket cash will total $2.5 million (25 × $100,000). Over the same 25 year period, the corporation will receive net tax deductions of $6.5 million calculated as follows:

| | |
|---|---|
| $13,516,800 | ($540,672 annual rent × 25) |
| −7,016,800 | ($11,016,800 total debt service less principal amortization of $4,000,000) |
| $ 6,500,000 | |

Assuming that the property has no depreciable basis in the corporation's hands before the sale and assuming further that the corporation is a 46 percent bracket taxpayer, on an after-tax basis, the $6.5 million in deductions will generate tax savings of $2.99 million, which exceeds the $2.5 million that it actually paid over the term of the lease. On a present value basis, as well as on an absolute dollar basis, the corporation's cost of money is reduced. Of course, by entering into this transaction the seller-lessee is giving up depreciation and residual value, and to that extent, the benefits of the purchase-money mortgage in the foregoing example are lessened.

The projected tax benefits of ownership, plus the rent paid by the lessee, plus the residual value of the real estate at the end of the lease term, represent a repayment to the lessor of the cost of the asset plus his desired return. Rent may be paid in a number of ways, ranging from monthly in advance to semian-nually in arrears.

The lease constant (the rent expressed as a percentage of the cost of the asset) and the absolute number of dollars paid by a lessee can be affected by the method of paying rent. For example, assume a situation where a seller-lessee and an institutional buyer-lessor agree on a sale-leaseback of the lessee's new office building, which as a cost of $10 million. The sale-leaseback is structured to give a return to the buyer-lessor of 10 percent. The buyer-lessor is willing to allow the lessee to pay rent on any basis he chooses. The following illustrates a number of possibilities and the annual dollars of rent that would be expended as rent:

| | |
|---|---|
| Monthly in advance | $1,081,429 |
| Monthly in arrears | 1,090,441 |
| Quarterly in advance | 1,065,829 |
| Quarterly in arrears | 1,092,475 |
| Semiannually in advance | 1,043,366 |
| Semiannually in arrears | 1,095,535 |
| Annually in advance | 1,001,528 |
| Annually in arrears | 1,101,681 |

The selection of the manner of payment can have a material effect on the actual dollars paid. Here it ranges from $1,001,528 (annually in advance) to $1,101,681 (annually in arrears). A lessee, depending on which alternative it chooses, is borrowing either more or less money. The business determination as to which alternative is most advantageous should take into consideration the lessee's cash flow, the flexibility of its credit lines, the alternative cost of money, and the rate at which money can be employed. If the lessee's alternative cost of money is greater than 10 percent, then to the extent allowed by its cash flow, it should pay rent in arrears. Rather than borrowing money from a bank at a higher rate, the lessee is effectively borrowing it from the lessor at 10 percent. If, on the other hand, the lessee's cost of money is less than 10 percent, it may be better off choosing an advance form of payment. By following this route, the lessee is effectively borrowing less from the lessor and saving some expense in the way of current rental payments.

The manner of payment relates only to the fact that the lessee may borrow short-term funds to bridge the advance/arrears differential. It does not affect the ultimate decision regarding the sale-leaseback itself.

## TAX ASPECTS OF A SALE-LEASEBACK

Assuming that a corporation has determined that in its particular circumstances a sale-leaseback is a desirable transaction, it is important that the transaction be treated for tax purposes as a true lease, rather than as a loan or a financing arrangement. The consequences of an adverse determination would result in the disallowance to the lessee of a deduction for rent and a disallowance of depreciation to the buyer-lessor.

The seller-lessee should attempt to place itself economically in a position as close to actual ownership as the buyer-lessor and the tax laws will allow. In this regard, the lessee will want to:

1   Control the property for as long as possible.
2   Have the flexibility to deal with the property in any way it chooses.
3   Have the ability to purchase the property at the lowest possible price during and after the lease term.

The seller-lessee, in attempting to achieve these objectives, should be aware of the basic principles of the tax law in this area.

The Internal Revenue Service's position is stated in Revenue Ruling 55-540, which sets forth, as the critical factor in determining whether a transaction is a true lease, the intent of the parties as evidenced by the provisions of the agreement read in light of the facts and circumstances existing at the time the agreement was executed. (For a discussion of Revenue Ruling 55-540, see Chapter 3.)

To review, Revenue Ruling 55-540 considers a number of criteria, any one of which may indicate that the purpose of lessee was, in fact, to acquire an equity interest in the property—a factor that is inconsistent with a true lease. These criteria include:

1   Whether portions of the periodic payments are made specifically applicable to an equity interest to be acquired by the lessee.
2   Whether the lessee will acquire the title on payment of a stated amount of rentals that he is required to make under the contract.
3   Whether the total amount the lessee is required to pay for a relatively short period of time constitutes an inordinately large proportion of the total sum required to be paid to secure the transfer of the title.
4   Whether the agreed rental payments materially exceed the current fair rental value (this may be indicative of the fact that the payments include an element other than compensation for the use of property).
5   Whether the property may be acquired under a purchase option for a price that is nominal in relation to the value of the property at the time when the option may be exercised, determined at the time the original agreement is entered into, or for a price that is relatively small when compared with the total payment required.
6   Whether some portion of the periodic payments is specifically designated as interest or is otherwise readily recognizable as the equivalent of interest.

The ruling also indicates that a security agreement in the nature of a conditional sales contract (an arrangement inconsistent with a true lease) will be presumed if the total of the rental payments together with the option price approximates the price (plus interest or carrying charges) at which the property could have been acquired by purchase at the time the agreement was entered into.

## PURCHASE OPTIONS

A great deal of tax litigation in the leasing area revolves around purchase options retained by the lessee. The most important factor usually is whether the option price established at the beginning of the term of the lease is so low in relation to the anticipated value at the time the option can be exercised that it is relatively certain that the option will be exercised. If the bargain element effectively mandates the exercise of the purchase option, the transaction will be characterized as something other than a true lease.

The courts view the ultimate determination as to whether a transaction is a true lease as a question of fact to be determined by the intention of the parties and the substance (as opposed to the form) of the transaction. In this connection, the courts will look to a number of other indicators in the transaction that will bear on its ultimate determination. Among these indicators, some of which are mentioned in Revenue Ruling 55-540, are the following:

1  *Rental payments applicable to purchase option price.* The courts have not necessarily found that rental payments that are applicable to the purchase price are fatal to the classification of a transaction as a lease. However, at least one court held against the finding of a lease because the rental payments were applied against the purchase price. Originally, the parties had agreed on the purchase price as an outright sales price.

2  *Rejectable offers to purchase versus options to purchase.* Some leases provide that if a particular property is no longer economically suitable for its intended use, the lessee can cancel its lease or offer to repurchase the property. It is critical from a tax standpoint that the offer to repurchase by the lessee be rejectable by the lessor. Absent the right to reject, the lessee can acquire property that has greatly appreciated in value for a use other than the one originally contemplated (e.g., an office building where a department store was previously located) at less than its fair market value.

3  *Treatment on the books and records of the parties.* Generally how the parties treat the transaction on their books is a very strong indication of their true intentions but it is not necessarily determinative, particularly in the case of bank leasing companies.

**4** *Sale and simultaneous leaseback for less than fair market value.* This factor, combined with other negative factors, may be indicative of a financing as distinguished from a lease in that one generally does not sell something at a bargain price except when one retains an equity interest. However, it is not uncommon for a seller-lessee to sell at depreciated book value to avoid tax on the sale.

**5** *Seller-lessee pays all the buyer-lessor's expenses.* Where the issue of the lease/purchase option is a close question, the payment of expenses can tip the scale; the situation is analogized to a loan where the borrower pays all the lender's expenses. This is not typical of a lease transaction.

**6** *Lessor's interest in refinancing the property.* When the lessor (as opposed to the lessee) has the right to refinance, the transaction will generally be held to be a true lease.

**7** *Possibility of gain.* The right of the lessee to participate in excess insurance proceeds, to the extent that such proceeds exceed the amount necessary to restore the facility to its prior condition, is inconsistent with its position as lessee. The same holds true when the lessee has the right to participate in condemnation proceeds that should be applicable to the lessor's estate.

**8** *Residual values.* It is generally necessary for the lessor to have some residual value in the property. For example, where the lessee has a 99 year lease, the courts have found that to be inconsistent with the finding of a true lease. Similarly, where the lessee owns land underlying a building as fee owner, it should grant the lessor of the building a substantial period of time over which it may control the land when the fee owner-lessee can no longer control the improvements. The period of time often set is 15 years.

The law and the ruling policy surrounding equipment leasing are much more definite than those involving real estate. Despite the fact that the Internal Revenue Service has indicated that its most recent pronouncements on leasing were intended only for equipment, it has also indicated that some of the principles may be equally applicable to real estate transactions.

Revenue Procedure 75-21, which deals with advanced ruling guidelines for leveraged leases (see Chapter 3), does not indicate the status of the tax law in the leasing area but only the criteria required to be met in order to obtain an advance ruling. Unlike Revenue Ruling 55-540, guidelines for Revenue Procedure 75-21 are not founded in case law. Failure to conform with the guidelines could precipitate an audit by the IRS, but that does not necessarily mean that an adverse determination will result.

The principal elements of Revenue Procedure 75-21 and their relevance to real estate are discussed as follows:

**1** *Minimum unconditional at risk investment of 20 percent at all times throughout lease investment.* This element is inconsistent with real estate sale-leasebacks, where high leverage financing has traditionally been available and 100 percent financings without any equity investment are common.

**2** *Fair market value at end of lease term equal to 20 percent original cost.* This element is directed at equipment, which is presumed to decline in value with the passage of time. Real estate transactions consist of an interest in land either by fee title or otherwise, which ordinarily does not depreciate but may appreciate substantially, making the 20 percent test difficult to calculate.

**3** *Lessee must not be able to purchase property at less than fair market value.* This element is inconsistent with legal precedents where a reducing fixed-price option has been permitted. However, the law indicates that at the time of the signing of the lease, the fixed-price option must be for a reasonable estimate of fair market value at the time the option can be exercised.

**4** *No investment or loan by lessee.* This element is inconsistent with the conventional real estate marketplace where a seller-lessee may take back a purchase money mortgage or where the seller-lessee may retain the fee and sell and lease back only the improvements.

**5** *Residual value must exceed initial equity plus reasonable cash flow from transaction.* The first element of this test is not unreasonable in its application to a real estate transaction although it has no foundation in case law. The second element is generally irrelevant to real estate because of the residual values inherent in the transaction and the possibility of creating a cash flow by refinancing during the course of the lease.

Unlike equipment lessees, which have traditionally relied on private rulings from the Internal Revenue Service, real estate lessees have rarely sought rulings but have, instead, relied on opinions of counsel. Theoretically, Revenue Procedure 75-21 should have little impact on most real estate transactions since the Internal Revenue Service has indicated the general inapplicability of the Revenue Procedure to real estate. However, the principles incorporated in the ruling may be applied on audit.

# Chapter 8

# PROJECT LEASE FINANCING

Project financing has sometimes been used to describe all types and kinds of financing of projects. The term is more precisely defined as:

> A financing of a particular economic unit in which a lender is satisfied to look to the cash flows and earnings of that economic unit as the principal source of funds from which a loan will be repaid and to the assets of the economic unit as collateral for the loan.

Project financing has more appeal when it does not have a significant impact on the balance sheet or the creditworthiness of a sponsoring company (the sponsor). Lease financing as a method of financing projects may be a means to accomplish the end of off-balance-sheet financing.

Industries engaged in the production, processing, transportation, or use of energy have been particularly attracted to project financing techniques because of the great needs of such companies for new sources of capital. The motivation for a project may be to make a profit. However, often the motivation for the project is to provide processing or distribution of a product of the sponsor or to insure a source of supply vital to the sponsor's business.

The goal in project financing is to arrange borrowing for a project that will benefit the sponsor and at the same time be nonrecourse to the sponsor, that is, not affecting its credit standing or balance sheet. In this sense, project financing is called "off-balance-sheet" financing. Off-balance-sheet financing can be accomplished by using the credit of a third party to support the transaction. However, infrequently projects are constructed or financed without credit support from sponsors or interested third parties.

There is considerable room for discussion between lenders and borrowers as to what constitutes a feasible project financing. Borrowers may prefer their projects to financed off balance sheet. Lenders, on the other hand, are just that, lenders. They are not in the venture capital business. Most of them do not want to be equity risk takers even if they are compensated as equity risk takers.

**141**

Lenders want to feel secure that they are going to be repaid either by the project, the sponsor, or a third party. This is the challenge of most project financings. The key to successful project financing is structuring the financing of a project with as little recourse as possible to the sponsor while at the same time providing sufficient credit support through guarantees of the sponsor or third party so that lenders will be satisfied with the credit risk.

There is a misconception that the term project financing means off-balance-sheet financing to the point that the project is completely self-supporting. This leads to misunderstandings and disappointments by prospective borrowers who may be under the impression that certain kinds of projects can be financed as project financings and, therefore, proceed on the assumption that similar projects in which they are interested can be financed completely nonrecourse, off balance sheet, and without any additional credit support. Credit support of a substantial nature is required in any project financing.

## CHARACTERISTICS OF A VIABLE PROJECT FINANCING

An independent economic unit that qualifies as a viable credit for a project financing will usually be backed by a strong credit. This credit backing may be provided by the sponsor or by a third party. The credit backing may be for the construction and start-up period only rather than for the life of the project. It may take the form of direct or indirect guarantee, take-or-pay contracts, or economic necessity contracts. These types of supports can be structured so that they do not have the same impact as debt on the sponsor's balance sheet. The supports may be off balance sheet for the sponsor if support is provided by a third party. Optimistic prospects for a project and/or the collaterial value of a project are insufficient alone to support a financing.

The financial viability of a project financing must be shown. Conservative projections of cash flows should be prepared and justified by independent feasibility and engineering studies. The cash flow projections must be sufficient to service debt, provide for cash needs, pay operating expenses, and still provide an adequate fund for contingencies.

Supply contracts for a project must be indicated at a cost consistent with the financial projections. A market for the product or service must be indicated at a price consistent with the financial projections. If take-or-pay contracts are being relied on, they must be written tightly.

Transportation for supplies and raw materials into the project and transportation for the output of the project must be indicated at a cost consistent with financial projections. The experience of the contractor who is to construct the facility must be well established. The financial capability to cover cost overruns and complete the project so that it operates in accordance with cost and production specifications must be available.

The project should not be a new technology. The reliability of the process and the equipment to be used should be well established. The technical reliability and commercial viability of the project should also be well established. If a new technology is involved, more than a lending risk is involved; therefore, institutional lenders will not be interested in the project.

The sponsor of the project should have available the expertise to operate the facility. The project cannot be a start-up situation that depends on going to the outside to hire the expertise to operate the new facility. In addition to operating expertise, management personnel should be available to manage the project. If the sponsor is deficient in managment personnel, the project is suspect.

## CAUSES FOR PROJECT FINANCING FAILURES

It is best to appreciate the concerns of lenders to a project by reviewing causes for project failures:

1  Delays in completion with consequent delay in the revenue flow.
2  Capital cost overrun.
3  Technical failure.
4  Financial failure of the contractor.
5  Government interference.
6  Uninsured casualty losses.
7  Increased price or shortages of raw materials.
8  Technical obsolescence of the plant.
9  Loss of competitive position in the market place.
10  Expropriation.
11  Poor management.

For a project financing to be viable, these risks must be addressed properly.

## CREDIT IMPACT OBJECTIVE

Although the sponsor or the beneficiary of a project financing ideally would prefer a nonrecourse borrowing that does not affect its credit standing or balance sheet, many project financings are directed toward achieving particular objectives such as the following objectives to:

1  Avoid showing the project on the face of the balance sheet.
2  Avoid showing the project as debt on the face of the balance sheet so that financial ratios are unaffected.

3  Avoid showing the project in a particular footnote to the balance sheet.
4  Avoid showing the project within the scope of restrictive covenants in an indenture or loan agreement that may preclude direct debt financing or leases for the project.
5  Avoid an open-end first mortgage.

Any one or a combination of these objectives may be sufficient reason for a borrower to seek the structure of a project financing.

Where a sponsor or a beneficiary of a project initially cannot arrange non-recourse borrowings that will not have an impact on its balance sheet, the project still may be feasible if the sponsor is willing to assume the credit risk during the construction and start-up phase and provided lenders are willing to shift the credit risk with respect to the project after the project facility is completed and operating. Under such an arrangement, most of the objectives of an off-balance-sheet project financing can be achieved after the initial risk period of construction and start-up. In some instances, lenders may be satisfied to look to unconditional take-or-pay contracts from users of the product or services to be provided by the project. In other instances, the condition of the market for the product or service may be such that sufficient revenues are assured after completion of construction and start-up so that lenders can rely on such revenues for repayment of their debts.

## ACCOUNTING CONSIDERATIONS

The purpose of a project financing is to segregate the credit risk of the project so that the credit risk of lending to the sponsor as distinct from the project can be clearly appraised. The purpose is not to hide or conceal a liability of the sponsor from creditors, rating services, or stockholders.

Since project financings are concerned with balance sheet reporting, familiarity with accounting terms is important. Terms such as contigent liability, indirect liability, deferred liability, deferred expense, and materiality are used to rationalize the appropriate positioning of entries on sponsors' balance sheets. Accounting rules for reporting liabilities are under continual review as the accounting profession grapples with the problem of proper and fair disclosure and presentation of objective information to stockholders, lenders, government agencies, and other concerned parties.

## TAX AND OTHER CONSIDERATIONS

Tax benefits from investment tax credit, depreciation, interest deductions, depletion deductions, and noncapital start-up expenses are significant considerations in the investment, debt service, and cash flow of project financings. Consideration must be taken in structuring a project financing to ensure that these benefits are utilized. Since often for such projects, a new entity is created—one that does not have taxes to shelter—it is important to shift available tax benefits to the parties that can currently use them.

There are often other benefits that result from segregating a financing as a separate project that may have a bearing on the motives of the company seeking a project financing. For example,

1  Credit sources may be available to the project that would not be available to the sponsor.
2  Guarantees may be available to the project that would not be available to the sponsor.
3  A project financing may enjoy better credit terms and interest costs in situations in which a sponsor's credit is weak.
4  Legal requirements applicable to certain investing institutions may be met by the project but not by the sponsor.
5  Regulatory problems affecting the sponsor may be avoided.
6  For regulatory purposes, costs may be segregated clearly as a result of a project financing.
7  The project may enable a sponsor in a regulated industry to achieve certain objectives regarding its rate base.
8  Investment protection in foreign projects may be improved through joint ventures with international parties.
9  A favorable labor contract or climate may be possible by separating the operation from other activities of the sponsor.

There are many methods of undertaking a project financing, including mortgage or debenture bonds, nonrecourse debt, leveraged leases, and joint ventures. Since this book is oriented to lease finance, the remainder of this chapter will be devoted to leveraged leasing as a vehicle for project finance.

## LEASES

The use of a lease to finance all the equipment and facilities of a project may in itself convert the financing into a project financing since many of the objectives of a project financing can be achieved by using a lease.

Apart from the use of leasing to achieve a project financing of capital equipment, leases may be used in conjunction with numerous project financing structures, which makes knowledge of leasing important to understanding the potential of many kinds of project financing.

There are two types of lessors involved in project financing: (1) third party leasing companies and (2) sponsors or parties interested in the completion of a project. Third party leasing companies are engaged in the finance business and offer an outside source of funds to finance projects. Third party leasing company rates are often more attractive than those of many alternative sources of funds due to the fact that in "true lease" financing the lessor claims tax benefits that are passed through to the lessee in the form of lower cost lease rentals.

### Tax Aspects of Leases

The Internal Revenue Service distinguishes between two basic forms of lease agreements.

First, the leveraged or nonleveraged true-leases to which most of the following discussion pertains. Tax benefits associated with ownership of the leased property may be claimed by a lessor under a true lease.

Second, a type of finance lease that the Internal Revenue Service treats as a conditional sale contract. In such a lease, the lessor holds legal title to the equipment throughout the lease term but the lease term may be for the full economic life of the equipment or the lessee may have an option to purchase the equipment at the end of the lease for a nominal price. In such cases the IRS regards the lessee as owner of the equipment from the beginning of the lease. The lessee may claim depreciation deductions and investment tax credit, but can deduct only the interest portion of the "rent" payments. Likewise, the lessor is treated for tax purposes as though it receives interest income. When a governmental agency, such as a city or state is the lessee, there is an interesting result; which is defined as a tax-exempt lease. This is becoming a popular means of financing government projects.

The lease that qualifies as a "true lease" for tax purposes is the type of lease to which most of the benefits commonly attributable to leasing apply. Under a "true lease," the lessor owns the equipment during and at the end of the lease term. The lessor claims depreciation deductions and the lessee may deduct the full lease payments for tax purposes. Investment tax credits may be claimed by the lessor or—by agreement—the lessee. where a third party is the lessor, most of the tax benefits claimed by the lessor are passed through to the lessee in the form of lower rents. This is the primary attraction of leasing as a financing device.

We discussed the requirements for a true lease in Chapter 3.

### True Leases: Direct and Leveraged

Leases that are true leases fall into two categories: (1) nonleveraged leases (also called direct leases) and (2) leveraged leases. The leveraged form of a true lease is the ultimate form of lease financing. Leveraged leasing has developed over the past few years to satisfy a need for lease financing of especially large capital equipment projects with economic lives of up to 25 years. The leveraged lease can be a most advantageous financing device when used for the proper projects and structured properly. Leveraged leases can also be used by sponsor lessors to leverage their lease investment. The concept of the leveraged lease is quite similar to that of the nonleveraged lease, but it is more complex in terms of size, number of parties involved, and unique advantages to these parties.

The primary difference between a leveraged and nonleveraged lease is that in a nonleveraged lease the lessor provides 100 percent of the capital from its own funds, while in a leveraged lease the lessor becomes the owner of the equipment by providing only a percentage (20 to 40 percent) of the necessary capital. The remainder of the capital in a leveraged lease is borrowed from institutional investors on a nonrecourse basis. This loan is secured by a first lien on the propery and equipment, an assignment of the lease, and an assignment of the lease rental payments.

The cost of the nonrecourse borrowing is a function of the credit standing of the lessee. The lease rate varies with the debt rate and with the risk of the transaction.

The lessor can claim all tax benefits incidental to ownership of the leased asset even though the lessor provides only 20 to 40 percent of the capital needed to purchase the asset.

The leverage created by the nonrecourse debt in a leveraged lease produces tax shelter in respect to the lessor's equity investment. Therefore, leverage is a two-edged sword for the lessor. Although it magnifies tax shelter, it also magnifies risk.

## Parties to a Leveraged Lease

Leveraged leases are complex from a legal and tax standpoint. A number of parties are involved. The functions of the parties are different. The lessee selects, operates, and receives all income from use of the asset, and the lessee makes rental payments. The equity participants provides the equity contribution (20 to 40 percent of the purchase price) to purchase the asset. The equity participants also receive rents remaining after payment of debt service, taxes, and trustee fees, if any, and claim the tax benefits incidental to the ownership of the leased asset. The equity participants are referred to as the lessors. Actually, in most cases, they are beneficial owners by way of an owner trust that is actually the lessor in legal terms. Equity participants may be referred to as equity holders, owner participants, or trustors. The lenders (debt holders or loan participants) are typically banks, insurance companies, trusts, pension funds, and foundations. The funds provided by the lendors together with the equity contributions make up the full pruchase price of the asset to be leased. The lenders provide 60 to 80 percent of the purchase price on a nonrecourse basis to the equity participants, and they receive debt service out of rents directly from the indenture trustee.

## LEVERAGED LEASES

An owner trust is established by the equity participants; trust certificates are issued, and a lease agreement is signed by the owner trustee lessor and the lessee. A security agreement is signed by the owner trustee and the indenture trustee; a mortgage is granted on the leased asset and the lease and rentals are assigned as security to the indenture trustee.

Notes or bonds are issued by the owner trustee to the lenders; debt funds are paid by the lenders to the indenture trustee; equity funds are paid by the equity participants to the indenture trustee. The purchase price is paid and title is assigned to the owner trustee, subject to the mortgage. The lease commences. Rents are paid by the lessee to the indenture trustee. Debt service is paid by the indenture trustee to the lenders. Revenue not required for debt service or trustees' fees is paid to the owner trustee and, in turn, to the equity participants. The owner trustee holds title to the leased asset for the benefit of the equity participants subject to a mortgage in favor of the indenture trustee. The owner trustee issues trust certificates to equity holders evidencing the equity holders' beneficial interest as owners of the assets of the trust, issues bonds to debt holders, grants to the indenture trustee the security interests that secure repayment of the bonds (i.e. lease, lease rentals, and first mortgage on the leased asset), receives distributions from the indenture trustee, and distributes earnings to the equity participants. Additional practical reasons for having an owner trustee from the standpoint of the lessors are: insulating liability on the bonds and avoiding regulatory red tape involved in the issuance of securities. The indenture trustee receives funds from lenders and equity holders, pays the purchase price of the equipment subject to its security interest (mortgage), holds the security interest in the leased equipment for the benefit of the lenders, and receives rents and other sums due under the lease from the lessee. The indenture trustee also pays the debt service and distributes revenues not needed for debt service to the owner trustee. In the event of default, the indenture trustee can forclose on the asset. The manufacturer or supplier of equipment receives the purchase price and delivers the equipment.

### Structure of a Leveraged Lease

A leveraged lease transaction is structured as follows where a third party bank leasing company or lease broker arranges the transaction.

The bank leasing company or broker arranging the lease contacts the prospective lessee and obtains a commitment letter for the lease of the equipment on certain terms, including the timing and amount of rent payments. Since the exact rent payment cannot be determined until the debt is placed, rents are agreed on based on various assumed debt rates.

After the commitment letter is signed, the broker contracts and arranges for a firm equity commitment from equity participants to the extent that the broker does not intend to provide equity funds from its own resources. The broker also arranges the debt either directly or in conjunction with an investment banker. If the equipment is not delivered for a considerable period of time, the debt may not be arranged until shortly before delivery or completion of the facility.

If an owner trustee is utilized, a bank or trust company acceptable to both the lessors and lessee is selected to act as owner trustee. Again, if utilized, another bank or trust company acceptable to the debt holders is selected to act as indenture trustee. On small transactions, a single trustee may act as both owner trustee and indenture trustee.

Exhibit 7.2 illustrates the cash flow and agreements between the parties.

If the leveraged lease is arranged by sponsors of a project who want to be the lessors, the structure and procedure is essentially the same as a leveraged lease by a third party lessor. In such a situation, the sponsors are the equity investors.

If some of the sponsors can use tax benefits and some cannot use tax benefits, the equity participants may include a combination of sponsors and one or more third party leasing companies. This is somewhat more complex, but the structure and procedure is essentially the same as a leveraged lease by a third party lessor. Internal Revenue guidelines for tax rulings do not permit leases to related parties.

When the parties to the transaction have been identified, all (except in some cases the indenture trustee) enter into a financing agreement or participation agreement that specifies in detail the various undertakings, obligations, indemnities, and responsibilities of the parties with respect to providing funds and purchasing, leasing, and mortgaging the equipment.

When the transaction is about to close, the equity participants pay the amount of their equity investments to the indenture trustee. The debt holders also pay the amount they are lending on the transaction to the indenture trustee. The owner trustee then issues equity participation certificates to the equity holders and bonds and debt certificates to the bondholders or debt holders.

Simultaneously, a lease agreement for the equipment has been signed between the owner trustee (as lessor) and the lessee. The indenture trustee has recorded a security interest or mortgage on the equipment to be leased. The lease agreement, the right to receive rents under it, and a mortgage on the equipment are assigned to the indenture trustee as security for the debt holders under a security agreement between the owner trustee and the indenture trustee.

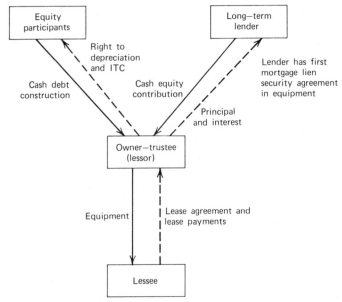

*Exhibit 7.1* Leveraged Lease Agreement

At the closing of the purchase of the equipment, the lessee signifies his acceptance of the equipment by signing an acceptance certificate. The indenture trustee páys the purchase price for the equipment to the manufacturer and to any construction lenders. Title is then conveyed to the owner trustee, subject to the previously recorded security agreement and mortgage. The equipment is delivered to the lessee, and the lease commences.

The lessee pays rents to the indenture trustee, who uses such funds to pay principal and interest payments to the bondholders. The balance of the rent payments is paid to the owner trustee. After payment of any trustee fees and expenses, the remaining income is paid to the equity participants.

The lease agreement ususally requires the lessee to furnish the owner trustee and indenture trustee with financial statements, convenant compliance data, evidence of insurance, and other similar information. The trustees distribute this information to all parties to the transaction.

Leveraged leases are capital leases (direct financing leases) that have the following additional characteristics:

1 Three parties (lessor, lessee, long-term lender).
2 Long-term debt that is nonrecourse to the lessor.

**3** Lessor investment that typically declines during the early years of the lease and rises during the later years of the lease.

The lessor in a leveraged lease recognizes income differently than for a direct lease. The lessor records his investment net of the nonrecourse debt (which the lessor does not report as debt on its balance sheet). Net after-tax cash receipts received from the lease, less the original investment by the lessor, represent the net income from the lease. The expected rate of return on the net investment in the lease, in the years in which such investment is positive, is computed by using projected cash receipts and disbursements, and such yield is applied to the net investment to determine periodic income to be recognized, with income assigned to those periods in which the net investment is positive.

A lease that does not meet the criteria for a capital lease (that is, a direct financing lease or a sale-type lease) must be accounted for as an operating lease.

Accounting for a lease as an operating lease is generally not acceptable to a lessor engaged in the business of long-term leasing because of the resultant deferral of income.

In a situation in which the lessee wants a lease classified as an operating lease in order to keep the lease off its balance sheet and/or out of its income statement, except as rental expense, a potential conflict exists over the classification of the lease since the third party lessor will, in nearly all cases, want to record the lease as a capital lease.

There is, however, no requirement that a lease classified as an operating lease for the lessee must also be classified as an operating lease for the lessor.

It is sometimes possible to structure a lease that will qualify as an operating lease for the lessee and as a capital lease for the lessor. For example, a lease that is clearly an operating lease can be changed to a capital lease on the books of the lessor without affecting the classification as an operating lease on the books of the lessee through the expedient of the lessor entering into a contractual arrangement with an independent third party for a guarantee of the residual value or renewal of the lease term. However, guaranteed residual values are contrary to Internal Revenue Service guidelines for true lease tax rulings. A lessor and a lessee may also report the same lease as a capital lease and an operating lease, respectively, by using different interest rates in determining the present value of minimum lease payments. The lessor using the rate of interest implicit in the lease and the lessee using its incremental borrowing rate. The lessor and lessee may arrive at different classifications because they reach different conclusions on judgmental issues, such as the estimated economic life, lease terms, and bargain purchase options. The latter is the most common reason for disparity in treatment of leases by lessees and lessors. Finally, substantial lessors may be able to avoid conflict on the grounds of immateriality in their total financial picture.

As discussed previously, most of the economic benefits commonly associated with leasing are available only in a true lease. The requirements for a true lease are easier to meet than the financial accounting requirements for classifying a lease as an operating lease. Although nearly all operating leases are true leases, only some capital leases qualify as true leases.

For many reasons, leasing from a third party lessor is attractive as a source of financing. However, each company's situation is different. Factors favoring leasing in one case may not be applicable in another case. Any one of the following advantages may be significant enough to cause leasing to be the most attractive financing alternative in a given situation.

**Low Cost and Inability of Lessee to Make Efficient Use of Tax Benefits.**

The most important factor favoring leasing is its lower cost. This is especially true where for one reason or another a lessee cannot take advantage of tax benefits, such as depreciation, interest, and investment tax credits. In such situations, a lessor able to use tax benefits can purchase the equipment, claim the tax benefits, lease the equipment to the lessee, and pass through most of the tax benefits to the lessee in the form of lower lease rates.

Nominee companies used to operate project financings that do not generate much taxable income are ideal candidates for lease financing. A joint venture in which some of the parties to the joint venture are not in a tax-paying position is also a candidate for lease financing.

Compared to a loan, lease payments can provide a lessee with more favorable cash flows during the first years of use of the leased equipment. Furthermore, the overall cash flows on a present-value basis are often more attractive in a lease.

**Joint Venture**

Leasing is beneficial for joint venture partnerships in which tax benefits are not available to one or more of the partners because of the way in which the joint venture is structured or because of the tax situation of one or more of the joint venture partners. In such cases, the lessor utilizes the tax benefits that would otherwise be lost and passes those benefits through to the joint venturers in the form of lower lease payments.

**Project Financing**

Leasing works well for project financings structured through subsidiaries not consolidated for tax purposes and consequently not in a position to claim and use tax benefits from equipment acquisitions. Lease payments can be timed to coincide with throughput, burn, and usage payments. Leases can be supported by take-or-pay or throughput contracts.

Some projects can be structured so that the lessor will take title to the equipment throughout construction with interest expense capitalized into the lease when the equipment is completed and delivery accepted by the lessee. A lease can be structured to be on or off balance sheets for financial accounting purposes, in accordance with the accounting objectives of the lessee and other cost tradeoffs the lessee is willing to make to achieve such objectives. During the years of a lease, rentals under a properly structured lease will usually have less impact on book earnings than depreciation and interest payments associated with the purchase of the same equipment. Depending on the language and intent of covenants in existing loan and note agreements, a lease may provide a method of financing when other types of financing are not permitted under such restrictions.

A predetermined fixed rent payment schedule permits a lessee to predict future equipment financing costs and cash needs more accurately than if the equipment is owned outright. In addition, by leasing major equipment items, a lessee knows the exact amount of future payments and avoids the risks inherent in fluctuations in the cost of funds. A lessee under an operating lease may be able to amortize the cost of equipment faster through tax deductible rentals than through depreciation and after-tax cash flow. Future rents for equipment acquired through a lease based on today's price will be paid in inflated dollars. A lessor can borrow long to protect itself from inflationary trends and provide this pro tection to a lessee in the form of long-term level lease payments. Within certain limits, payment schedules can be designed to coincide with earnings generated from equipment use, with seasonal activity patterns, or with projected business growth. Because the timing of lease payments can be arranged to track normal business cycles, leasing offers a flexibility that may not be available with other financing methods.

Leasing is often simply more convenient than alternative means of financing. Documentation, particularly in the $1 million to $5 million dollar size transaction, can be simpler and more flexible than other sources of capital, such as debt placement and equity.

Public disclosure of financial information and confidential trade information is not required for a lease transaction. Such information is required in a prospectus for a public offering of debt or equity, and it is sometimes required in a private offering prospectus.

Leasing provides 100 percent financing (which may include shipping and installation charges), while a typical equipment loan requires an initial down payment.

A lease may ultimately cost more than a purchase in terms of total dollars in cases where the lessee can currently use tax benefits of ownership. However, a lease permits retention of capital that can be utilized elsewhere in the lessee's business. Additional earnings can be generated from this retained capital making the overall cost of leasing more attractive. Most costs incurred in acquiring equip ment can be structured into the lease and amortized over the life of the lease. These costs include delivery charges, interest charges on advance payments, sales or use taxes, and installation costs. Such charges are usually not financed under alternative methods of equipment financing.

Acquisition of equipment not contemplated in a capital expenditure budget can sometimes be accomplished through use of a lease with lease payments structured so that they can be classified as an operating expense. Where the costs of plant and equipment expected to be financed by industrial revenue bonds exceed statutory limits, equipment can often be acquired through a lease to keep the remainder of the project within the bond limits.

An "open-end" first mortgage restriction (which precludes purchase of ad ditional equipment unless it is included under the mortgage) can sometimes be avoided by acquiring the use of such equipment under a lease. Some public utilities have such "open-end" first mortgage restrictions.

Since lease obligations are not "securities" as defined by the Interstate Commerce Act, railroads and other companies subject to ICC securities provi sions can avoid obtaining ICC approval and competitive bidding by leasing. Dilution of ownership of a company from issuance of equity or con vertible securities can be avoided through use of a lease for needed equipment.

A company that places emphasis on ROA (return on assets) will find operating leases attractive and off-balance-sheet structures utilizing leases attractive.

Where a lessee is in a foreign tax credit carryforward position or an ITC carryforward position, lease rentals will have less adverse impact then depre ciation and interest expense on claiming tax benefits from such carryforwards.

Where a lessee is required to reflect interest on a construction loan during construction as an income statement expense item, this effect can be avoided by an agreement to lease the equipment on completion on a basis whereby the lessor takes title to the property during construction and capitalizes construction interest into the cost of the equipment.

## Appendix A

# SUMMARY OF AMENDMENTS TO AND INTERPRETATIONS OF FASB NO. 13

**FASB NO. 17**

**Accounting for Leases—Initial Direct Costs**

*Issued November 1977; Effective January 1, 1978*

Amends paragraph 5(m) of FASB No. 13 to read as follows:

> *Initial Direct Costs*   Those costs incurred by the lessor that are directly associated with negotiating and consummating completed leasing transactions. Those costs include, but are not necessarily limited to, commissions, legal fees, costs of credit investigations, and costs of preparing and processing documents for new leases acquired. In addition, that portion of salespersons' compensation, other than commissions, and the compensation of other employees that is applicable to the time spent in the activities described above with respect to completed leasing transactions shall also be included in initial direct costs. That portion of salespersons' compensation and the compensation of other employees that is applicable to the time spent in negotiating leases that are not consummated shall not be included in initial direct costs. No portion of supervisory and administrative expenses or other indirect expenses, such as rent and facilities costs, shall be included in initial direct costs.

**FASB NO. 22**

### Changes in the Provisions of Lease Arrangements Resulting from Refundings of Tax-Exempt Debt

*Issued June 1978; Effective July 1, 1978*

Allows a change in the provisions of the lease arrangement that results from a refunding of tax-exempt debt to be treated in accordance with APB Opinion No. 26, Early Extinguishments of Debt.

**FASB NO. 23**

### Inception of the Lease

*Issued August 1978; Effective December 1, 1978*

Under FASB Statement No. 13, Accounting for Leases, the *inception of the lease* is the date on which the classification of a lease is determined. The lease is recorded at the beginning of the lease term using the classification that was determined at the date of the inception of the lease. If the property covered by a lease is yet to be constructed or has not yet been acquired by the lessor at the date of the lease agreement or any earlier commitment, this Statement:

1 Changes the "inception of the lease" from the date that construction is completed or the property is acquired by the lessor to the date of the lease agreement or any earlier commitment. This change is intended to result in a lease classification that more closely reflects the substance of the transaction.

2 Changes the lessee's determination of "fair value of the leased property" for a lease with a cost-based or similar escalator provision from the amount estimated on the inception date to an amount that is escalated to give effect to increases under the escalator clause when:

    **(a)** Fair value is used as a limitation of the amount of the asset to be recorded.

    **(b)** Fair value is used as a basis for allocation of recorded amounts between land and buildings.

This change is intended to base the lessee's accounting on amounts that relate to the finally determined lease payments.

If the redefined "inception of the lease" is a date before the beginning of the lease term, with limited exceptions this Statement prohibits the recording of increases in estimated residual value that may occur between those two dates.

## FASB NO. 26

### Profit Recognition on Sales-Type Leases of Real Estate

*Issued April 1979; Effective August 1, 1979*

This Statement specifies that a lease of real estate that would otherwise be classified as a sales-type lease under FASB Statement No. 13, Accounting for Leases, and that results in a "sales-type" profit shall be classified as an operating lease by the lessor unless at the beginning of the lease term it also meets the conditions for full and immediate profit recognition as described in the *AICPA Industry Accounting Guide*, "Accounting for Profit Recognition on Sales of Real Estate." This means that a lessor would be precluded from classifying a lease as a sales-type lease and recognizing a "sales-type" profit unless, for example, the lessor receives lease payments as of the beginning of the lease in an amount at least equal to the minimum down payment requirement specified by the *AICPA Industry Accounting Guide*. The down payment requirements of the Guide range from 5 to 25 percent depending on the type of property. The Statement does not affect the classification of a sales-type lease of real estate that results in a "sales-type" loss, nor does it affect the classification of a lease of real estate that would be classified as a direct financing lease.

## FASB NO. 27

### Classification of Renewals or Extensions of Existing Sales-Type or Direct Financing

*Issued May 1979; Effective September 1, 1979*

This Statement modifies FASB Statement No. 13, Accounting for Leases, to require a lessor to classify a renewal or an extension of a sales-type or direct financing lease as a sales-type lease if the lease would otherwise qualify as a sales-type lease and the renewal or extension occurs at or near the end of the lease term. If the renewal or extension occurs at other times during the lease term, the prohibition in FASB Statement No. 13 against classifying the renewal or extension as a sales-type lease continues in effect. Furthermore, this Statement does not affect the classification of a lease that results from a change in the provisions of an existing lease or the accounting for changes in the provisions of a lease if those changes occur during the lease term.

## FASB NO. 28

### Accounting for Sales with Leasebacks

*Issued May 1979; Effective September 1, 1979*

Paragraph 33 of *FASB Statement No. 13*, Accounting for Leases, generally treats a sale-leaseback as a single financing transaction in which any profit or loss on the sale is deferred and amortized by the seller, who becomes the lessee. This Statement requires the seller to recognize some profit or less in either of the following limited circumstances:

1   If the seller retains the use of only a minor part of the property or a minor part of its remaining useful life through the leaseback, the sale and the lease would be accounted for based on their separate terms. However, if the rentals called for by the lease are unreasonable in relation to current market conditions, an appropriate amount would be deferred or accrued by adjusting the profit or loss on the sale. The amount deferred or accrued would be amortized as an adjustment of those rentals.

2   If the seller retains more than a minor part but less than substantially all the use of the property through the leaseback and the profit on the sale exceeds the present value of the minimum lease payments called for by the leaseback for an operating lease or the recorded amount of the leased asset for a capital lease, that excess would be recognized as profit at the date of the sale.

## FASB NO. 29

### Determining Contingent Rentals

*Issued June 1979; Effective October 1, 1979*

This Statement defines contingent rentals as the increases or decreases in lease payments that result from changes occurring subsequent to the inception of the lease in the factors on which lease payments are based. Lease payments that depend on a factor that exists and is measurable at the inception of the lease, such as the prime interest rate, would be included in minimum lease payments based on the factor at the inception of the lease. Lease payments that depend on a factor that does not exist or is not measurable at the inception of the lease, such as future sales volume, would be contingent rentals in their entirety and, accordingly, would be excluded from minimum lease payments and included in the determination of income as they accrue.

# FASB INTERPRETATION NO. 19

## Lessee Guarantee of the Residual Value of Leased Property

*Issued October 1977; Effective January 1, 1978*

Interprets FASB No. 13 as follows:

1   A lease provision requiring the lessee to make up a residual value deficiency that is attributable to damage, extra wear and tear, or excessive usage is similar to contingent rentals.

2   If a lease limits the amount of the lessee's obligation to make up a residual deficiency to an amount less than the stipulated residual value of the leased property at the end of the lease term, the amount of the lessee's guarantee to be included in minimum lease payments is limited to the specified maximum deficiency the lessee can be required to make up.

3   A guarantee of the residual value obtained by the lessee from an unrelated third party for the benefit of the lessor shall not be used to reduce the amount of the lessee's minimum lease payments except to the extent that the lessor explicity releases the lessee from obligation to make up a residual value deficiency.

# FASB INTERPRETATION NO. 21

## Accounting for Leases in a Business Combination

*Issued April 1978; Effective May 1, 1978*

Provides that the classification of a lease in accordance with the criteria of FASB No. 13 shall not be changed as a result of a business combination unless the provisions of the lease are modified. In a poolings of interest, each lease retains its previous classification under FASB No. 13 and is accounted for in the same manner that it would have been classified and accounted for by the acquirer. In a purchase acquisition, the leases retain their previous classification; however, the amounts assigned to individual assets and liabilities assumed shall be determined in accordance with the provisions of paragraph 88 of APB No. 16, which requires measurement of the assets and liabilities at fair value.

## FASB INTERPRETATION No. 23

### Leases of Certain Property Owned by a Governmental Unit or Authority

*Issued August 1978; Effective December 1, 1978*

This Interpretation clarifies that portion of paragraph 28 of FASB Statement No. 13, Accounting for Leases, stating that leases of certain property owned by a governmental unit or authority shall be classified as operating leases. The Interpretation describes six conditions that must be met for a lease of government owned property to be automatically classified as an operating lease. If all six conditions are not met, the criteria for classifying leases under FASB No. 13 that are applicable to leases generally are also applicable to leases involving government owned property.

## FASB INTERPRETATION NO. 24

### Leases Involving Only Part of a Building

*Issued September 1978; Effective December 1, 1978*

This Interpretation concerns that portion of FASB Statement No. 13, Accounting for Leases, stating that "when the leased property is part of a larger whole, its cost (or carrying amount) and fair value may not be objectively determinable, as for example, when an office or a floor of a building is leased."

This Interpretation recognizes that reasonable estimates of the leased property's fair value might be objectively determinable from other information if sales of property similar to the leased property do not exist.

## FASB INTERPRETATION NO. 26

### Accounting for Purchase of a Leased Asset by the Lessee During the Term of the Lease

*Issued September 1978; Effective December 1, 1978*

This Interpretation clarifies the application of paragraph 14 of FASB Statement No. 13, Accounting for Leases, to a termination of a capital lease that results from the purchase of a leased asset by the lessee.

The purchase by the lessee of property under a capital lease and the related lease termination are accounted for as a single transaction. The difference, if any, between the purchase price and the carrying amount of the lease obligation is recorded as an adjustment of the carrying amount of the asset. The Board also noted that FASB No. 13 does not prohibit recognition of a loss if a loss has been incurred.

## FASB INTERPRETATION NO. 27

### Accounting for a Loss on a Sublease

*Issued November 1978; Effective March 1, 1979*

This Interpretation clarifies that recognition of a loss by an original lessee who disposes of leased property or mitigates the cost of an existing lease commitment by subleasing the property is not prohibited by FASB Statement No. 13, Accounting for Leases.

This Interpretation also clarifies the treatment of a sublease that is part of a disposal of a segment. The determination of a gain or loss on disposal of the segment, under the provisions of APB Opinion No. 30, Reporting the Results of Operations, comprehends amounts related to an original lease and a sublease entered into as part of the decision to dispose of the segment. Any gain or loss on the sublease becomes an indistinguishable part of the gain or loss on the disposal.

# FASB TECHNICAL BULLETINS

December 28, 1979                                No. 79-10

# FASB Technical Bulletin

| | |
|---|---|
| **Title:** | Fiscal Funding Clauses in Lease Agreements |
| **Reference:** | FASB Statement No. 13, *Accounting for Leases,* paragraph 5(f) |

## Question

1. What effect, if any, should the existence of a fiscal funding clause in a lease agreement have on the classification of the lease under Statement 13?

## Background

2. A fiscal funding clause is commonly found in a lease agreement in which the lessee is a governmental unit. A fiscal funding clause generally provides that the lease is cancelable if the legislature or other funding authority does not appropriate the funds necessary for the governmental unit to fulfill its obligations under the lease agreement.

## Response

3. Paragraph 5(f) of Statement 13 requires that a cancelable lease, such as a lease containing a fiscal funding clause, be evaluated to determine whether the uncertainty of possible lease cancellation is a remote contingency. That paragraph states that "a lease which is cancelable (i) only upon occurence of some *remote* contingency . . . shall be considered 'noncancelable' for purposes of this definition" of lease term. (Emphasis added.)

4. In discussing the likelihood of the occurrence of a future event or events to confirm a loss contingency, paragraph 3 of FASB Statement No. 5, *Accounting for Contingencies*, defines *remote* as relating to conditions when "the chance of the future event or events occurring is slight." The evalu-

ation of the uncertainty of possible lease cancellation should be consistent with that definition.

5.  The existence of a fiscal funding clause in a lease agreement would necessitate an assessment of the likelihood of lease cancellation through exercise of the fiscal funding clause. If the likelihood of exercise of the fiscal funding clause is assessed as being remote, a lease agreement containing such a clause would be considered a noncancelable lease; otherwise, the lease would be considered cancelable and thus classified as an operating lease.

# FASB Technical Bulletin

**Title:** Effect of a Penalty on the Term of a Lease

**Reference:** FASB Statement No. 13, *Accounting for Leases*, paragraph 5(f)

## Question

1. In determining the lease term under the provisions of Statement 13, does the existence of a penalty that would reasonably assure renewal of a lease need to be stated in the lease agreement?

## Background

2. Paragraph 5(f) of Statement 13 states that the lease term includes "all periods, if any, for which failure to renew the lease imposes a penalty on the lessee in an amount such that renewal appears, at the inception of the lease, to be reasonably assured."

## Response

3. The "penalty" referred to in paragraph 5(f) of Statement 13 is not limited to a penalty imposed by the lease agreement. Accordingly, the lease term would also include any periods for which failure to renew the lease would result in an economic penalty as a result of factors external to the lease so long as (a) the existence of the penalty were known at the inception of the lease and (b) the nature and estimated amount of the penalty at the inception of the lease were such that renewal would appear to be reasonably assured.

# FASB Technical Bulletin

| | |
|---|---|
| **Title:** | Interest Rate Used in Calculating the Present Value of Minimum Lease Payments |
| **Reference:** | FASB Statement No. 13, *Accounting for Leases,* paragraphs 5(l) and 7(d) |

## Question

1. May a lessee use its secured borrowing rate in calculating the present value of minimum lease payments in applying the provisions of Statement 13?

## Background

2. Paragraph 7(d) of Statement 13 requires the lessee to use its incremental borrowing rate (or the lessor's implicit interest rate in certain circumstances) to calculate the present value of minimum lease payments. The incremental borrowing rate is defined in paragraph 5(l) as "the rate that . . . the lessee would have incurred to borrow over a similar term the funds necessary to purchase the leased asset."

## Response

3. Paragraph 5(l) of Statement 13 does not proscribe the lessee's use of a secured borrowing rate as its incremental borrowing rate if that rate is determinable, reasonable, and consistent with the financing that would have been used in the particular circumstances.

# FASB Technical Bulletin

**Title:**        Applicability of FASB Statement No. 13 to Current Value Financial Statements

**Reference:**   FASB Statement No. 13, *Accounting for Leases*, paragraphs 7 and 8

## Question

1. Are financial statements prepared on a current value basis exempt from the provisions of Statement 13?

## Response

2. Statement 13 would not be inapplicable merely because financial statements are prepared on a current value basis. For example, if at its inception a lease involving property meets one or more of the four criteria of paragraph 7 and both of the criteria of paragraph 8 of Statement 13, the lessor would classify the lease as a sales-type or direct financing lease, whichever is appropriate. Subsequently, the carrying amount of the recorded investment in the lease payments receivable would be adjusted in accordance with the valuation techniques employed in preparing the financial statements on a current value basis.

# FASB Technical Bulletin

---

**Title:** Upward Adjustment of Guaranteed Residual Values

**Reference:** FASB Statement No. 13, *Accounting for Leases,* paragraphs 17(d), 18(d), and 46

## Question

1. Does the prohibition against upward adjustments of estimated residual values in Statement 13 also apply to upward adjustments that result from renegotiations of the guaranteed portions of residual values?

## Background

2. Paragraphs 17(d), 18(d), and 46 of Statement 13 require the lessor to review annually the estimated residual value of sales-type leases, direct financing leases, and leveraged leases, respectively. Those paragraphs also contain a provision that prohibits any upward adjustment of the estimated residual value.

## Response

3. The prohibitions of paragraphs 17(d), 18(d), and 46 of Statement 13 against upward adjustments to the leased property's estimated residual value are equally applicable to the guaranteed portion. If a lease initially transferred substantially all of the benefits and risks incident to the ownership of the leased property, it would not seem appropriate that the lessor could subsequently increase the benefits that were accounted for as having been retained initially.

4. Recording upward adjustments to the leased property's residual value would, in essence, result in recognizing a sale of the residual value interest. In this respect, the prohibition of

169

an upward adjustment in the leased property's residual value is similar to the prohibition in paragraph 17 of FASB Statement No. 5, *Accounting for Contingencies,* of recognizing gain contingencies because to do so might be recognizing revenue before realization. Realization of the residual value interest might also be contingent on factors, such as the physical condition of the leased property or the requirements and related costs, if any, relating to remarketing agreements at the end of the lease term.

# FASB Technical Bulletin

**Title:**          Accounting for Loss on a Sublease Not Involving the Disposal of a Segment

**References:**    FASB Statement No. 13, *Accounting for Leases,* paragraphs 35-39
FASB Interpretation No. 27, *Accounting for a Loss on a Sublease*

## Question

1. Should a loss on a sublease not involving the disposal of a segment be recognized and how is it determined?

## Response

2. The general principle of recognizing losses on transactions and the applicability of that general principle to contracts that are expected to result in a loss are well established. Accordingly, if costs expected to be incurred under an operating sublease (that is, executory costs and either amortization of the leased asset or rental payments on an operating lease, whichever is applicable) exceed anticipated revenue on the operating sublease, a loss should be recognized by the sublessor. Similarly, a loss should be recognized on a direct financing sublease if the carrying amount of the investment in the sublease exceeds the total of rentals expected to be received and estimated residual value unless the sublessor's tax benefits from the transaction are sufficient to justify that result.

3. The absence of explicit reference to accounting for these

transactions in Statement 13 does not affect the necessity to follow general principles of loss recognition.

# FASB Technical Bulletin

| | |
|---|---|
| **Title:** | Effect of a Change in Income Tax Rate on the Accounting for Leveraged Leases |
| **Reference:** | FASB Statement No. 13, *Accounting for Leases,* paragraph 46 |

## Question

1. What effect, if any, does a change[1] in the income tax rate have on the accounting for leveraged leases under Statement 13?

## Background

2. Paragraph 46 of Statement 13 provides that, when an important assumption changes, the rate of return and the allocation of income shall be recalculated from the inception of the lease, and the change in the recalculated balances of net investment shall be recognized as a gain or loss in the year in which the assumption is changed.

## Response

3. The lessor's income tax rate is an important assumption in accounting for a leveraged lease. Accordingly, the income effect of a change in the income tax rate should be recognized in the first accounting period ending on or after the date on which the legislation effecting a rate change becomes law.[2]

---

[1]FASB Technical Bulletin No. 79-16 addressed the effect of a reduction in the corporate income tax rate from 48 percent to 46 percent. Because the response is applicable to increases as well as decreases in the tax rate, this revised Bulletin has been generalized to address the effect of all income tax changes on the accounting for leveraged leases.

[2]Bulletin 79-16 stated "ending on or after the *effective date of the rate change.*" (Emphasis added.) This revised Bulletin clarifies the ambiguity of that phrase.

4. If accounting for the effect on leveraged leases of the change in tax rates results in a significant variation from the customary relationship between income tax expense and pretax accounting income and the reason for that variation is not otherwise apparent, paragraph 63 of APB Opinion No. 11, *Accounting for Income Taxes*, requires that the reason for that variation should be disclosed.

# FASB Technical Bulletin

---

**Title:**    Reporting Cumulative Effect Adjustment from Retroactive Application of FASB Statement No. 13

**Reference:**    FASB Statement No. 13, *Accounting for Leases,* paragraph 51

## Question

1. If a company presents in its annual report five annual income statements that were retroactively restated to apply the provisions of paragraphs 1-47 of Statement 13, must the cumulative effect of applying those provisions be included in determining net income of any period presented?

## Background

2. Paragraph 49 of Statement 13 requires retroactive application of the provisions of that Statement in financial statements for fiscal years beginning after December 31, 1980. Financial statements presented for prior periods are to be restated. Paragraph 51 of that Statement requires that the cumulative effect on the retained earnings at the beginning of the earliest period restated shall be included in determining the net income of that period.

## Response

3. The cumulative effect of applying the provisions of paragraphs 1-47 of Statement 13 would *not* be included in net income of any period presented unless the year prior to the earliest year presented could not be restated. Paragraph 51 does not refer to the earliest period *presented* but rather refers to the earliest period *restated*. Thus, if income statements for five years are presented and the next prior year cannot be restated, the cumulative effect would be included

in the determination of net income of the first year presented. In that same situation, if a company presented income statements only for the current year and the immediately preceding year, neither income statement would include a cumulative effect adjustment.

# FASB Technical Bulletin

| Title: | Transition Requirement of Certain FASB Amendments and Interpretations of FASB Statement No. 13 |
|---|---|
| References: | FASB Statements 17, 22, ·23, 26, 27, 28, and 29<br>FASB Interpretations 19, 21, 23, 24, 26, and 27<br>[All related to FASB Statement No. 13, *Accounting for Leases*] |

## Question

1. In applying the transition requirement of the amendments and interpretations of Statement 13, what is meant by the phrase "have published annual financial statements" and what disclosure is required to indicate that Statement 13 had been applied retroactively without restatement of the prior years' financial statements due to immateriality?

## Background

2. The relevant portion of the transition requirement in FASB amendments and interpretations of Statement 13 states:

> In addition, except as provided in the next sentence, the provisions of this [Interpretation/Statement] shall be applied retroactively at the same time and in the same manner as the provisions of FASB Statement No. 13 are applied retroactively (see paragraphs 49 and 51 of Statement No. 13). Enterprises that *have already applied the provisions of Statement No. 13 retroactively and have published annual financial statements* based on the retroactively adjusted accounts before the effective

date of this [Interpretation/Statement] may, but
are not required to, apply the provisions of this
[Interpretation/Statement] retroactively. [Empha-
sis added.]

## Response

3. The phrase "have published annual financial statements"
generally refers to those financial statements that a company
normally includes in its annual report to shareholders for its
established 12-month reporting period (that is, its fiscal
year). Inclusion of the word "published" in the transition
requirement emphasizes that the annual financial statements
should be those that are distributed to all shareholders. For
a publicly held company, those financial statements would
normally be accompanied by an independent auditor's
opinion.

4. Although the phrase "have published annual financial
statements" generally refers to the financial statements
included in a company's annual reports to shareholders,
other circumstances, such as in a filing under the requirements of the Federal Securities Act, may necessitate the
issuance to all shareholders of complete financial statements
for a company's established 12-month reporting period.
For example, if a calendar-year company files a registration
statement with the Securities and Exchange Commission
in October 1978 and subsequently delivers a proxy statement
containing complete financial statements for its year ended
December 31, 1977 to all shareholders, the 1977 financial
statements (which would include all footnotes contained in
the annual report to shareholders) that are included in the
proxy statement could constitute published annual financial
statements as contemplated by the transition requirement
of the amendments and interpretations of Statement 13.

5. On the other hand, the "have published annual financial
statements" provision would not be met if the calendar-year
company referred to in the above example included its 1977

financial statements, restated to adopt the requirements of Statement 13 retroactively, in the 1978 third quarter interim report to shareholders unless inclusion of its normal fiscal year financial statements is consistent with that company's previously established reporting practices. In addition, the issuance of complete financial statements for a 12-month period that is not the company's established fiscal year would not constitute published annual financial statements for purposes of satisfying the transition requirement in question.

6. Amendments and interpretations of Statement 13 should be applied retroactively as they become effective unless Statement 13 had been applied retroactively in published annual financial statements to shareholders at an earlier date. The retroactive application of Statement 13 would not necessarily require the recording of an adjustment in a company's accounting records when the effects of applying Statement 13 on a retroactive basis call for adjustments that are clearly immaterial. However, in those instances, it could be expected that the notes to the published annual financial statements would have included appropriate disclosure to indicate that the company had adopted Statement 13 retro-actively and that prior years' financial statements were not restated because the effects of retroactive application were immaterial. The absence of such disclosures would indicate that Statement 13 had not yet been adopted retroactively. Similarly, if the notes to financial statements in an annual report to shareholders include the "as if" disclosures required by paragraph 50 of Statement 13, it would also be apparent that a company had not adopted the provisions of Statement 13 on a retroactive basis in those earlier financial statements.

# GLOSSARY OF LEASE TERMS

*ADR—Asset Depreciation Range*   Regulations under the Internal Revenue Code Section 167(m) that permits shorter or longer usual lives to be used for tax depreciation. Under certain circumstances, capital assets may be depreciated over a period that may be up to 20 percent longer or shorter than the applicable class life, rounded to the nearest half year.

*Bargain Purchase Option*   A provision allowing the lessee, at his or her option, to renew a lease for a rental sufficiently lower than the expected fair market value at the time such option becomes exercisable, such that exercise of the option appears, at the inception of the lease, to be reasonably assured.

*Bargain Renewal Option*   A provision allowing the lessee, at his or her option, to renew the lease for a rental sufficiently lower than the expected fair rental for the property at the time the option becomes exercisable, such that the exercise of the option appears, at the inception of the lease, to be reasonably assured.

*Bonds*   Certificates evidencing indebtedness or loan certificates issued by the owner trustee.

*Broker*   A company or person who arranges lease transactions between lessees and lessors for a fee.

*Burdensome Buyout*   A provision in a lease allowing the lessee to purchase leased property at a value to be determined in some fashion when the buyout is exercised, in the event that payments under the tax or general indemnity clauses are deemed by the lessee to be unduly burdensome. Care must be taken that the existence of such a provision does not invalidate the true lease nature of the transaction and thus by its existence make the lessee liable under the tax indemnity clause.

*Burn up Contract*   Another name for a nuclear fuel lease.

*Call*   An option to purchase an asset at a fixed price at some particular time in the future. Care must be used in negotiating a purchase option or call in a lease agreement. If this is done improperly, many of the advantages of a true lease may be disallowed by the Internal Revenue Service.

*Capital Lease*   A lease is classified and accounted for by a lessee as a capital lease if it meets any of the following criteria:

1   The lease transfers ownership to the lessee at the end of the lease term.
2   The lease contains an option to purchase property at a bargain price.
3   The lease term is equal to 75 percent or more of the property (except for used property leased in last 25 percent of its useful life).
4   The present value of minimum lease rental payments is equal to 90 percent or more of the fair market value of the leased property less related ITC retained by the lessor (does not apply for used property leased in last 25 percent of its useful life).

*Casualty Value*   See *Insured Value*.

*Certificate of Acceptance*   A document whereby the lessee acknowledges that the property to be leased has been delivered to him or her, is acceptable to him or her, and has been manufactured or constructed in accordance with specifications.

*Collateral*   Collateral under a lease is the property that is leased.

*Conditional Sale*   A transaction for purchase of an asset in which the user, for federal income tax purposes, is treated as the owner of the property at the outset of the transaction.

*Conditional Sale Lease*   A lease that in substance is a conditional sale (sometimes called a hire-purchase agreement).

*Contingent Rentals*   Rentals in which the amounts depend on some factor other than passage of time.

*Debt Service*   Payments of principal and interest due lenders.

*Direct Financing Lease*   A nonleveraged lease by a lessor (not a manufacturer or dealer) in which the lease meets any of the criteria definitions of a *capital* lease, plus two additional criteria, as follows:

1   Collectibility of minimum lease payments must be reasonably predictable.
2   No uncertainties surround the amount of unreimbursable costs to be incurred by the lessor under the lease.

*Direct Investor*   Refers to the lessor in a direct financing lease.

*Direct Lease*   Same as a *direct financing lease*.

*Economic Life of Leased Property*   The estimated period during which the property is expected to be economically usable by one or more users, with normal repairs and maintenance, for the purpose for which it was intended at the inception of the lease.

*Equity Participant*   The lessor or one of a group of lessors in a leveraged lease. Equity participants hold trust certificates evidencing their beneficial interest as owners under the owner trust. An equity participant is the same as an owner participant, trustor owner, or grantor owner.

*Estimated Residual Value of Leased Property*   The estimated fair value of the property at the end of the lease term.

*Extended Term Agreement*   An agreement to renew a lease, commonly used to describe a guaranteed renewal of a lease by a third party.

*Fair Rental*   The expected rental for equivalent property under similar terms and conditions.

*FASB*   Financial Accounting Standards Board.

*FASB No. 13*   Technically: Statement of Financial Accounting Standards No. 13, Accounting for Leases, (Financial Accounting Standards Board, Stamford, Connecticut, November 1976.) Sets forth financial accounting standards on accounting for leases.

*Finance Lease*   A financing device whereby a user can acquire use of an asset for most of its useful life. Rentals are net to the lessor, and the user is responsible for maintenance, taxes, and insurance. Rent payments over the life of the lease are sufficient to enable the lessor to recover the cost of the equipment plus a return on its investment. A finance lease may be either a *true lease* or a *conditional sale*.

*Financing Agreement*   An agreement between the owner trustee, the lenders, the equity participants, the manufacturer, and the lessee that spells out the obligations of the parties under a leveraged lease. Also called *participation agreement*.

*Floating Rental Rate*   Rental that is subject to upward or downward adjustments during the lease term. Floating rents sometimes are adjusted in proportion to prime interest rate or commercial paper rate changes during the term of the lease.

*Grantor Trust*   A trust used as the owner trust in a leveraged lease transaction, usually with only one equity participant. The Internal Revenue Code refers to such a trust as a grantor trust (See Section 671). With more than one equity participant the grantor trust is usually treated as a partnership.

*Heat Supply Contracts*   A nuclear fuel lease.

*Hell-or-High-Water Clause*   A clause in a lease that stipulates the unconditional obligation of the lessee to pay rent for the entire term of the lease, regardless of any event affecting the equipment or any change in the circumstance of the lease.

*Hire-Purchase Agreement*   A conditional sale lease.

*Inception of a Lease*   The date of the lease agreement or the commitment, if earlier. (For technical application, consult FASB No. 13 and subsequent amendments.)

*Incremental Borrowing Rate*   The interest rate a company would expect to pay for an additional borrowing at rates prevailing at that time for a purchase of property similar to that which is being leased.

*Indemnity Agreement*   An agreement whereby the lessee indemnifies the trustees from liability as a result of ownership of the leased equipment.

*Indemnity Clause*   Although lease documentation contains various indemnities, the indemnity clause usually refers to the tax indemnity clause whereby the lessee indemnifies the lessor against the loss of tax benefits.

*Indenture Trustee*   In a leveraged lease, the indenture trustee holds the security interest in the leased property for the benefit of the lenders. In the event of default, the indenture trustee exercises the rights of a mortgagee. The indenture trustee also is responsible for receiving rent payments from the lessee and using such funds to pay the amounts due the lenders with the balance being paid to the owner trustee. The indenture trustee verifies that correct filings are made to protect the security interest of the lenders. The bond register is maintained by the indenture trustee, which also acts as transfer agent.

*Indenture of Trust*   An agreement between the owner trustee and the indenture trustee whereby the owner trustee mortgages the property and assigns the lease and rental payments under the lease as security for amounts due to the lenders. Similar to a security agreement or mortgage.

*Independent Lessor*   Any leasing company investing in leases; also, brokers without funds to invest in leases sometimes prefer to call themselves "independent lessors" rather than "brokers."

*Initial Direct Costs*   Costs incurred by a lessor that are directly associated with negotiating and completing a transaction. These include commissions, legal fees, costs of credit checkings, documentation costs, allocable sales expenses (including salaries other than commissions), and so forth, but specifically exclude supervisory, administrative, or other indirect or overhead expenses.

*Institutional Investors*   Investors such as banks, insurance companies, trusts, pension funds, foundations, and educational, charitable, and religious institutions.

*Insured Value*   A schedule included in a lease stating that the agreed value of property at various times during the term of the lease and establishing the liability of the lessee to the lessor in the event the leased property is lost or rendered unusable during the lease term, due to a casualty.

*Interest Rate Implicit in a Lease*   The discount rate that, when applied to *minimum lease payments* (excluding executory costs paid by the lessor) and *unguaranteed residual value,* causes the aggregate present value at the beginning of the lease term to be equal to the fair value of the leased property at the inception of the lease, minus any investment tax credit retained by the lessor and expected to be realized by him or her.

*Interim Rent*   Daily rental accruing from delivery, acceptance, and/or funding until a later starting date for a basic lease term. Often used when property is delivered over a period of time.

*ITC*   Investment Tax Credit.

*Lease Line*   A lease line of credit similar to a bank line of credit that allows a lessee to add property, as needed, under the same basic terms and conditions without negotiating a new lease.

*Lease Rate*   The equivalent simple annual interest rate implicit in minimum lease rentals. Not the same as *interest rate implicit in a lease.*

*Lease Term*   The fixed, noncancelable term of the lease. Includes, for accounting purposes, all periods covered by fixed-rate renewal options that for economic reasons are likely to be exercised at the inception of the lease and, for tax purposes, all periods covered by fixed-rate renewal options.

*Lease Underwriting*   An agreement whereby a packager commits firmly to enter into a lease on certain terms and assumes the risk of arranging any financing.

*Lessee*   The user of the property being leased.

*Lessee's Incremental Borrowing Rate*   The interest rate that the lessee at the inception of the lease would have incurred to borrow over a similar term the funds necessary to purchase the leased assets. In a leveraged lease, the rate on the lessor's debt is normally used.

*Lessor*   The owner of equipment that is being leased to a lessee or user.

*Level Payments*   Equal payments over the term of the lease.

*Leverage*   An amount borrowed. A lease is sometimes referred to as 100 percent leverage for the lessee. In a leveraged lease, the debt portion of the funds used to purchase the asset represents the leverage of the equity holder.

*Leveraged Lease*    A lease that meets the definition criteria for a *direct financing lease* or a *capital lease* and has the following characteristics:

1  At least three parties are involved: a lessee, a lessor, and a long-term lender.
2  The financing provided by the lender is substantial to the transaction and without recourse to the lessor.
3  The lessor's net investment typically declines during the early years of the lease and rises during the later years of the lease.

*Loan Certificates*    Debt certificates or bonds issued by the owner trustee to lenders.

*Loan Participant*    A lender in a leveraged lease; a holder of debt in a leveraged lease evidenced by loan certificates or bonds issued by the owner trustee.

*Master Lease*    A lease line of credit that allows a lessee to add property under the same basic terms and conditions without negotiating a new lease contract.

*Minimum Investment*    For a leveraged lease to be a *true lease,* the lessor must have a minimum "at risk" investment of at least 20 percent in a lease when the lease begins, ends, and at all times during the lease term.

*Minimum Lease Payments for the Lessee*    All payments the lessee is obligated to make or can be required to make in connection with leased property, including residual value guarantees and bargain renewal rents or purchase options, but excluding guarantees of lessor's debt and executory costs such as insurance, maintenance, and taxes.

*Minimum Lease Payments for the Lessor*    The payments considered minimum lease payments for the lessee plus any guarantee by a third party of the residual value or rental payments beyond the lease term.

*Mortgage*    An agreement between the owner trustee and the indenture trustee whereby the owner trustee assigns title to the equipment as security for amounts due the lenders.

*Net Lease*    In a net lease, the rentals are payable net to the lessor. All costs in connection with the use of the equipment are to be paid by the lessee and are not a part of the rental. For example, taxes, insurance, and maintenance are paid directly by the lessee. Most capital leases and direct financing leases are net leases.

*Operating Lease*    For financial accounting purposes, a lease that does not meet the criteria of a capital lease or direct financing lease. Also, used generally to describe a short-term lease whereby a user can acquire use of an asset for a fraction of the useful life of the asset. The lessor may provide services in connection with the lease such as maintenance, insurance, and payment of personal property taxes.

*Owner Participant*   The lessor or one of a group of lessors in a leveraged lease holding trust certificates evidencing their beneficial interest as owners under the owner trust. An owner participant is the same as an equity participant, trustor owner, or grantor owner.

*Owner Trustee*   Also sometimes called grantor trustee. In a leveraged lease, the primary function of the owner trustee is to hold title to the equipment for the benefit of the equity participants. The owner trustee issues trust certificates to the equity participants, maintains the register, and acts as transfer agent for such certificates. The owner trustee issues notes to the lenders, receives distributions of rent payments from the indenture trustee, pays trustee fees due, and disburses amounts due the equity participants. The owner trustee makes appropriate filings to perfect and protect the lenders' interest in the collateral. Compliance certificates and other information required from the lessee under the lease are received by the owner trustee and distributed by the owner trustee to the other parties.

*Participation Agreement*   An agreement between the owner trustee, the lenders, the equity participants, the manufacturer, and the lessee that spells out the obligations of the parties under the leveraged lease. Also called *financing agreement*.

*Present Value*   The current equivalent value of cash available immediately for a future payment or a stream of payments to be received at various times in the future. The present value will vary with the discount (interest) factor applied to the future payments.

*Purchase Option*   An option to purchase leased property at the end of the lease term. In order to protect the tax characteristics of a true lease, an option to purchase property from a lessor by a lessee cannot be at a price less than its fair market value at the time the right is exercised.

*Put*   An option to sell an asset at a set price at some established point in time in the future. In lease agreements, a lessor sometimes negotiates an option to sell leased equipment to the lessee or to some third party at an established price at the end of the lease term. Care must be used in negotiating a put to a lessee lest the true lease characteristics of the transaction be destroyed and money-saving advantages lost. A lessor may also negotiate a put to a third party as a hedge against future loss on the sale of the asset, although such an arrangement is contrary to IRS advance ruling guidelines.

*Related Parties*   In leasing transactions: a parent and its subsidiaries; an investor and its investees; provided the parent, owner, or investor has the ability to exercise significant influence over the financial and operating policies of the related party.

**Renewal Option**   An option to renew the lease at the end of the initial lease term. Care must be used in granting a renewal option. If this is not done properly, it may later be ruled that the lease is not a true lease. Tax advantages may be lost and tax indemnity clauses activated.

**Residual Insurance**   An insurance policy guaranteeing a certain residual value at the end of the lease term.

**Residual or Residual Value**   The value of equipment at the conclusion of the lease term. To qualify the lease as a "true lease" for tax purposes, the estimated residual value at the end of the lease term must equal at least 20 percent of the original cost of the equipment.

**Residual Sharing**   An agreement between the lessor and another party providing for a division of the *residual value* between them. Care must be taken in any such agreement, lest the tax benefits be lost and the lessee become liable under the tax *indemnity clause*.

**Return on Investment**   The yield. The interest rate earned by the lessor in a lease that is measured by the rate at which the excess cash flows permit recovery of investment. The rate at which the cash flows not needed for debt service or payment of taxes amortize the investment of the equity participant.

**Revenue Procedures**   Commonly used in leasing to refer to the IRS Revenue Procedures 75-21, 75-28, and 76-30, which set forth requirements for obtaining a favorable revenue ruling on a leveraged lease.

**Revenue Ruling**   A written opinion of the Internal Revenue Service requested by parties that is applicable to assumed facts stated in the opinion. May also refer to published IRS rulings with general applicability.

**Sale-Leaseback**   A transaction involving the sale of the property by the owner and a lease of the property back to the seller.

**Sales-type Lease**   A lease by a lessor who is a manufacturer or dealer in which the lease meets the criteria of a *capital lease* and there is a manufacturer's or dealer's profit.

**Security Agreement**   An agreement between the owner trustee and the indenture trustee whereby the owner trustee assigns title to the property, the lease, and rental payments under the lease as security for amounts due the lenders. The same as an indenture of trust.

**Short-term Lease**   Generally, an operating lease.

**Sinking Fund**   A reserve or a sinking fund established or set aside for future payment of taxes (generally applicable only in leveraged leases).

*Sinking Fund Rate*   The rate of interest allocated to a *sinking fund* set aside for future payment of taxes (generally applicable only in leveraged leases).

*Special Purpose Property*   Property that is uniquely valuable to the lessee and is not valuable to anyone else except as scrap.

*Stipulated Loss Value*   The same as *insured value*.

*Sublease*   A transaction in which leased property is re-leased by the original lessee to a third party, and the lease agreement between the two original parties remains in effect.

*Strip Debt*   Debt in connection with a leveraged lease, arranged in tiers with different maturities to improve the lessor's cash flow and to reduce the lessee's costs.

*Termination Schedule*   Leases sometimes contain provisions permitting a lessee to terminate the lease during the lease term in the event the leased equipment becomes obsolete and surplus to its needs. In such event, the equipment usually must be sold or transferred to some third party unconnected in any way with the lessee. The liability of the lessee in the event of such termination is set forth in a termination schedule that values the equipment at various times during the lease term. If the equipment is sold at a price lower than the amount set forth in the schedule, the lessee pays the difference. In the event that the resale is at a price higher than in the termination schedule, such excess amounts belong to the lessor. The termination schedule is not the same as the *casualty value* schedule, *insured value* schedule, or *stipulated loss value* schedule.

*True Lease*   A transaction that qualifies as a lease under the Internal Revenue Code so that the lessee can claim rental payments as tax deductions and the lessor can claim tax benefits of ownership such as depreciation and ITC.

*Trust Certificate*   Document evidencing the beneficial ownership of a trust estate of an equity participant (or owner participant, trustor owner, or grantor owner) in an owner trust.

*Trustee*   A bank or trust company that holds title to or a security interest in leased property in trust for the benefit of the lessee, lessor, and/or creditors of the lessor. A leveraged lease often has two trustees: an owner trustee and an indenture trustee.

*Trust Fees*   Fees due either the owner trustee or the indenture trustee.

*Trustor Owner*   The lessor or one of a group of lessors under a leveraged lease holding trust certificates evidencing their beneficial interest as owners under the owner trust. A trustor owner is the same as an equity participant, owner participant, or grantor owner.

*Undivided Interest*   A property interest held by two or more parties whereby each shares, according to their respective interest, in profit, expenses, and enjoyment and whereby ownership of the respective interest of each may be transferred, but physical partition of the asset is prohibited.

*Unguaranteed Residual Value*   The portion of residual value "at risk" for a lessor in his or her yield computation, that is, the portion of residual value for which no party is obligated to pay.

*Useful Life*   The period of time during which an asset will have economic value and be usable. Useful life of an asset is sometimes called the economic life of the asset. To qualify as a true lease, the leased property must have a remaining useful life of 20 percent of the original estimated useful life of the leased property at the end of the lease term and a life of at least 1 year.

*Yield*   The interest rate earned by the lessor or equity participant in a lease, in which the excess cash flows permits recovery of investment. The rate at which the cash flows not needed for debt service or payment of taxes amortize the investment of the equity participants.

# BIBLIOGRAPHY

"Accounting Changes May Hit Leasing," *Building Owner and Manager*, **1** (September 1976), 1.

Adelmann, Richard L., "Alternative to Replacement Cost Accounting," *Financial Executive*, **45** (January 1977), 28–30.

Anderson, Paul F. and William Lazer, "Industrial Lease Marketing," *Journal of Marketing*, **42** (January 1978), 71–79.

Anderson, Paul F. and John D. Martin, "Lease vs Purchase Decisions: A Survey of Current Practice," *Financial Management*, **6** (Spring 1977), 41–47.

Benjamin, James J., S. Kerry Cooper, and Robert H. Strawser, "FASB Statement No. 13: Retrospect and Prospect," *CPA Journal*, **47** (June 1977), 79–81.

Beresford, Dennis R. and Robert D. Neary, "Interpretation Sheds Light on Residual Value Guarantee Accounting," *Financial Executive*, **45** (December 1977), 14.

Beresford, Dennis R. and Robert D. Neary, "SEC Wants to Speed Up Adoption of New Rules for Leases," *Financial Executive*, **45** (May 1977), 10.

Beresford, Dennis R. and Robert D. Neary, "Timing Tightened for New Lease Accounting Rules," *Financial Executive*, **45** (November 1977), 18.

Beresford, Dennis R. and John E. Rutzler, "New Accounting Rules for Leases," *California CPA Quarterly*, **45** (December 1977), 21–27.

Beresford, Dennis R. and Robert D. Neary, "Lessors' Initial Direct Costs Are Redefined," *Financial Executive*, **46** (January 1978), 12.

Bierman, Harold, "How Tax Rate Changes Affect the Lease-Purchase Decision," *Business Operations Tax Journal*, **1** (August 1976), 170–171.

Blake, Allen, "Insurance Company as Lessee." *Interpreter*, **36** (September 1977), 12–15.

Blake, Allen, "Insurance Companies as Leveraged Lessors," *Interpreter*, **36** (October 1977), 7–9.

Bovell, Steve A., "Subordinated Ground Lease," *Practical Lawyer*, **23** (September 1977), 12–15.

Bowles, G.N., "Some Thoughts on the Lease Evaluation Solution," *Accounting and Business Research*, **26** (Spring 1977), 124–126.

Burrows, G., "Lease Evaluation Solution: A Further Comment," *Accounting and Business Research*, **27** (Summer 1977), 208–210.

**191**

Burrows, Geoff H., "Lease Evaluation: The Saga Continues," *Australian Accountant*, **47** (August 1977), 437–438, 441–442.

Carty, J.P., "Accounting for Finance Leases: The Investment Period Method," *Accountant* **176** (January 20, 1977), 83–84, 87.

Colasanti, Matt, "Leasing Offers Many Advantages," *Credit & Financial Management*, **79** (January 1977), 34–35.

Darden, Richard T., "Real Estate Percentage Lease," *Journal of Property Management*, **42** (May/June 1977), 6–7.

Davis, Daniel N., "Real Estate Leasebacks from the Lessee's Point of View: An Economic and Tax Analysis," *Journal of Real Estate Taxation*, **3** (Summer 1976), 454–471.

Dyl, Edward A. and Stanley A. Martin, "Setting Terms for Leveraged Leases," *Financial Management*, **6** (Winter 1977), 20–27.

Dyl, Edward A., "Leasing Instead of Lending—An Approach to Lessor Rate Setting," *Journal of Commercial Bank Lending*, **59** (November 1976), 41–48.

Deming, John R., "Analysis of FASB No. 13," *Financial Executive*, **46** (March 1978), 46–51.

Eggleston, Charles H., "Don't Lease Bank Buildings," *Bankers Magazine*, **159** (Spring 1976), 81–84.

Englebrecht, Ted. D., "Replacement Clauses in Leases as a Tax Trap," *Real Estate Review*, **7** (Winter 1978), 14–15.

Etter, Wayne E., "Leverage and the Real Estate Investor," *Real Estate Review*, **7** (Fall 1977), 86–90.

Fawthrop, R.A. and Brian Terry, "Evaluation of an Integrated Investment and Lease-Financing Decision," *Journal of Business Finance & Accounting*, **3** (Autumn 1976), 79–111.

Fein, Zell Z., "Leasing Dilemma," *Motor Freight Controller*, (September 1977), 9–12.

Goldstein, Bernard H., "Value of Arbitration Provisions in Leases," *Practical Lawyer*, **22** (September 1, 1976), 53–60.

Goldstein, Bernard H., "When a Landlord Constructs or Alters Business Premises," *Practical Lawyer*, **23** (April 15, 1977), 59–72.

Grinyer, John R., "Lease Evaluation Solution: Continued," *Accounting and Business, Research*, **27** (Summer 1977), 211–214.

Halper, Emanuel B., "Uniform Landlord-Tenant Act Is Inadequate," *Real Estate Review*, **6** (Winter 1977), 86–91.

Haymes, Allan, "Making the Most of an Industrial Investment," *Real Estate Review*, **6** (Fall 1976), 14–17.

Hemmer, Edgar H., "Replacing the Bankrupt Shopping Center Tenant," *Real Estate Review*, **7** (Fall 1977), 57–61.

Henderson, Glenn V., "Decision Format for Lease or Buy Analysis," *Review of Business and Economic Research*, **12** (Fall 1976), 63–72.

Henry, James B., "Finding the True Cost of a True Lease," *Hospital Financial Management*, **6** (December 1976), 19–22, 24–25.

Hett, Frank, "How a Captive Leasing Company Can Create Tax Benefits for Vehicle or Equipment Dealer," *Taxation for Accountants*, **19** (July 1977), 32–38.

Kalata, John J., "Lease Financing Reporting," *Financial Executive*, **45** (March 1977), 34–40.

Kane, Howard E., "Landlord-Tenant Relationship in Bankruptcy," *Real Property, Probate and Trust Journal*, **12** (Fall 1977), 482–506.

Kasper, Larry J., "Evaluating the Cost of Financial Leases," *Management Accounting*, **58** (May 1977), 43–51.

"Lease Transfer to Partnership is One of Property Not Services," *Taxation for Lawyers*, **6** (January/February 1978), 220.

"Leaseback Arrangements Can Defer Recognized Gain," *Taxation for Lawyers*, **5** (November/December 1976), 169.

"Lease-Or-Buy Decision Reconsidered," *Journal of Accountancy*, **143** (June 1977), 81–88.

Marcus, Robert P., "Buy vs. Lease Decision Revisited," *Financial Executive*, **44** (December 1976), 34–38.

Meyers, Philip G., "Worksheet for Leasing Equipment," *Practical Lawyer*, **23** (July 15, 1977), 59–80.

Middleton, K.A., "Lease Evaluation: Back to Square One," *Accounting and Business Research*, **26** (Spring 1977), 127.

Milam, Robert D., "Suggested Conceptual Foundation for the Valuation of Partial Interests," *Appraisal Journal*, **45** (April 1977), 173–178.

Nessen, Robert L., "Band Premises: When to Own, When to Lease," *Banking*, **69** (June 1977), 49–51.

"New Rule May Force Some Banks to Capitalize Their Leased Premises," *Journal of Accountancy*, **145** (January 1978), 8.

Ofer, Sharon R. "Evaluation of the Lease Versus Purchase Alternatives," *Financial Management*, **5** (Summer 1976), 67–74.

Pakrul, Herb A., *Decision Maker's Perspective on How the Accounting System Can Meet User Needs,"* *Cost and Management*, **51** (September/October 1977), 12–19.

Papernick, Larry W. and F. Howard Henry, "Equipment Financing—the Leasing Alternative," *CA Magazine*, **110** (December 1977), 26–31.

Pond, Jonathan D., "Capitalizing Leased Assets," *Management Accounting*, **58** (January 1977), 45–47.

Prior, Robert E., "Putting Together the Office Lease," *Journal of Property Management*, **42** (November/December 1977), 301–303.

Regan, William J., "Dual Aspect of Leveraged Leasing," *Bankers Magazine*, **159** (Autumn 1976), 75–77.

Roenfeldt, Rodney L. and James B. Henry, "Lease vs. Debt Purchase of Automobiles," *Management Accounting*, **58** (October 1976), 49–54.

Schachner, Leopold, "New Accounting for Leases," *Financial Executive*, **46** (February 1978), 40–47.

Schloss, Nathan, "Inflation-Proofing Retail Investments with Percentage Leases," *Real Estate Review*, **7** (Winter 1978), 36–40.

Senchack, Andrew J. and James K. Malernee, "Reducing Risk in Financial Lease Commitments," *Risk Management*, **23** (September 1976), 32–33, 36–38.

Shanno, David F. and Roman L. Weil, "Separate Phases Method of Accounting for Leveraged Leases: Properties of the Allocating Rate and an Algorithm for Finding It," *Journal of Accounting Research*, **14** (Autumn 1976), 348–356.

Simon, William, "Leasing: What Should You Ask Your CPA?" *Financial Executive*, **45** (July 1977), 32–35.

Smith, Charles C., "Mortgaging the Leasehold," *Real Estate Review*, **7** (Fall 1977), 13–15.

Sorensen, Ivar W. and Roman E. Johnson, "Equipment Financial Leasing Practices and Costs: An Empirical Study," *Financial Management*, **6** (Spring 1977), 33–40.

Thompson, Earl G., "Some Tax Problems on Mid-Stream Modifications and Terminations of Leases," *Journal of Real Estate Taxation*, **4** (Spring 1977), 214–236.

# INDEX